MOK
WEI
WEI

Works by W Architects

MOK WEI WEI

Works by W Architects

Edited by Justin Zhuang

594 illustrations

Mok Wei Wei: Works by W Architects © 2020
Thames & Hudson Ltd, London

"'Totally Contextual': The Architecture of
Mok Wei Wei" © 2020 Chang Jiat-Hwee

"Architecture of the West and the East
Refracted through an Architect in Singapore"
© 2020 Leon van Schaik

For the illustrations, please see the
photographic credits list on page 352.

Edited by Justin Zhuang
Designed by Duet Design

First published in 2020 in the United States of
America by Thames & Hudson Inc., 500 Fifth
Avenue, New York, New York 10110

www.thamesandhudsonusa.com

Library of Congress Control Number
2019947912

ISBN 978-0-500-34345-6

Printed and bound in China by
Everbest Printing Investment Ltd

CONTENTS

02

03

DEDICATION

W Architects has its roots in William Lim Associates. Its founder William S. W. Lim's vision shaped the original practice founded in 1981, and his key values are still embraced today. It is my great privilege to have been mentored by William, and to have collaborated with him from 1982 to 2003.

W Architects could not maintain the quality of its works without Ng Weng Pan, a director since 2003. With his clarity of mind and considered approach, Weng Pan has been a worthy right hand at the practice. My gratitude, Weng Pan.

A special thanks to our staff, past and present, without whose talent and commitment the body of work presented in this book would not have been possible.

This book's cover is based on the top of the office's conference table, which we used for thirteen years from 1996 to 2009.

From the first day we had it, building-material samples with sharp edges began to leave indelible scratches on its medium-density-fibreboard (MDF) surface. While recognizing that it was probably an unsuitable choice of material, we saw a potential for the scratches to contribute to the design of the table and left it unprotected. Over a decade, the table top accumulated marks that recorded our time spent in that office. It even witnessed the firm's transition from William Lim Associates (WLA) to W Architects (WA) in 2003. Today, the table top is still with us but is displayed as a mural in the office.

PREFACE

I resisted the idea of doing a publication covering our projects for a long time, and this book only came about because of Lucas Dietrich, a director of Thames & Hudson, who turned up in our office one day in 2017, and has persistently pursued the scheme ever since. Documenting thirty-five years of our work has presented an opportunity to form an overview of our entire oeuvre, placing projects in the context of the times and environments in which they were conceived, and are still being made. Hopefully this approach will appeal to readers interested in following the path of a creative journey, and in understanding how ideas may be formed, developed, refined and even remade over time. On our part, putting the publication together has helped us recollect and reflect, which hopefully will give rise to greater focus and clarity for future works.

In reading about our projects, it is useful to know the evolution of the firm's structure. I first joined the boutique practice William Lim Associates (WLA) in the 1980s. This had been set up in 1981 by the pioneering Singaporean architect William S. W. Lim, who had just left a major practice that he co-founded in the late 1960s. In the 1990s, I became a partner in WLA, designing a range of works that were quite separate from Lim's, and it is these projects that form the focus of this book. When Lim retired in 2003, I continued to practise with the same team, and brought on a new partner, Ng Weng Pan, who had been with WLA since 1989. At this point, the firm was renamed W Architects (WA).

WA has practised almost entirely in Singapore, where, as in much of South and Southeast Asia, works are often labelled "Tropical Architecture". This term, which has its lineage in the colonialists' agenda for their tropical and subtropical outposts, has dominated the architectural discourse of the region. Today, it has morphed into something of global relevance – the pursuit of a green and sustainable architecture.

Our practice finds this term limiting, however, and we have avoided positioning our projects as such in this book. Instead, we trace the creative impetus and design approaches behind our works, which are not confined to climatic considerations. Over the following three chapters, we hope to demonstrate this, and contribute to expanding the architectural conversation in the region.

Chapter 01
Refract: In Search of Fundamentals

This chapter traces my personal search for creative directions from the early 1980s on. Crucially, this first decade of work also reflects the dynamics of the early collaboration between Lim and myself.

Chapter 02
Respond: Contextualism in a Constricting Environment

The dense city-state of Singapore has crafted its planning regulations so as to become a laboratory for high-density living in the Tropics. The works featured in this chapter are located entirely in Singapore, and outline the external forces that have shaped the practice's approach from the mid-1990s to today.

Chapter 03
Reflect: Negotiating Spatial Cultures in a Global City-State

As part of a Singapore society made up of diverse migrant cultures, the firm has looked inwards to find expressions for space-making. The works in this chapter also show how this young country has sped ahead to become a global city, while still trying to formulate a sense of self.

"TOTALLY CONTEXTUAL": THE ARCHITECTURE OF MOK WEI WEI[1]

By Chang Jiat-Hwee

The concept of context is hard to pin down because it always points to surrounding circumstances; context is the crucible in which buildings happen. Complicating this, context is at once a general and a specialized, disciplinary term. The same word appears prominently in two dissimilar realms: a common, casual usage where it can signify a set of immediate general conditions that help situate meaning, and a narrower professional field, where it evokes both current debate and a history still fresh from the 1970s.

Sandy Isenstadt[2]

"Context" is a word that kept appearing in my conversations with Mok Wei Wei. Once, he even said that many of his projects were "totally contextual". Mok is one of the most reflexive practitioners that I have encountered in Singapore. Speaking about his projects, he is always very conscious about what they were trying to achieve, why certain design decisions were made and how these were implemented in a consistent and meticulous manner. For Mok, the whats and whys of design are more than site and programmatic requirements; they often involve larger motivations, from personal design sensibilities to broader sociocultural impetuses. Given this centrality of "context" to Mok's oeuvre, I will discuss the various contexts that have shaped and might continue to shape his works.

However, as the epigraph suggests, "context" is a somewhat slippery and nebulous concept because of its multivalence. This essay embraces its many interpretations, and situates Mok's works in three overlapping sets of contexts. Starting with the personal and the generational context that informs his cultural and design sensibility, I then move on to discuss the architectural context of Postmodernism that backgrounded his first decade or so of practice. I end the essay by exploring the broader socio-economic context in the 1990s, which raised the value of design and allowed Mok and his practice to thrive from the middle of the decade. At the broadest level, these contexts represent the conditions of possibility that enable – without determining – Mok's designs. As Mok has built almost entirely in Singapore, this Southeast-Asian city-state inevitably forms the background to these various contexts. Thus, as with any place, Singapore requires context-ualizing, even though it is a global city. International architectural movements like Modernism and Postmodernism, and transnational socio-economic policies such as neoliberalism and globalization, were, and still are, mediated, translated and enacted differently in Singapore, reflecting its peculiarities. This essay is therefore not just an account of the contexts that shaped Mok's architecture, but also outlines the changing conditions of architectural production in Singapore over the past four decades.

The Personal and Generational Context of Chinese Cosmopolitanism

Mok's father is veteran journalist Mok Lee Kwang (莫理光) (b. 1926), who was the chief editor of Singapore's Chinese-language newspaper *Nanyang Siang Pau*. FIG. 1 Following the paper's merger with *Sin Chew Jit Poh* in the 1980s, he headed the amalgamated paper that resulted, *Lianhe Zaobao*, until his retirement in 1987. The senior Mok was also an avid art collector and was closely connected to prominent Chinese art and literary figures in Singapore, such as calligraphers and poets Pan Shou and Liu Beian (the latter's real name was Chua Boon Hean). Probably as a result of his father's extensive network of friends, the young Mok had the chance to witness Zhang Daqian – one of the best-known Chinese painters of the twentieth century – at work, and even received a piece from Zhang as a souvenir. Like his siblings, Mok was nurtured by his father in art and music. For many years, he was sent for lessons with the Singaporean artist Chen Wen Hsi, one of the pioneers of the Nanyang Style, and later was taught by Thomas Yeo, a prominent second-generation Singaporean artist known for his abstract compositions. Mok also had piano lessons for many years and obtained the Licentiate of the Royal School of Music before starting at university.[3]

The Second World War disrupted the education of Mok's father, as with so many of his generation. He was also diagnosed with tuberculosis at an early age and had to quit school before completing the ninth grade in junior high school. Without much formal education, the senior Mok moved up the ranks of the newsroom largely through hard work and self-education. Mok recalls seeing a copy of the French writer Romain Rolland's *Jean-Christophe* in his father's bookcase full of marginalia. The presence of this book by Rolland, who won the Nobel Prize in Literature in 1915, also hints at the cosmopolitan-ism of a generation of Chinese-educated art and literary figures in Singapore who, contrary to popular perception today, were neither parochial nor conservative.[4] For instance, one only needs to read the writings of the pioneering Nanyang painter and art educator Chen Chong Swee or the educator and art historian Marco Hsü to see how conversant they

FIG. 1 Mok Lee Kwang, *c.* 1950s.

1 This essay is informed by four long conversations with Mok on 12 December 2017, 24 June 2018, 6 July 2018 and 28 August 2018. The author would like to thank him for these informative and stimulating conversations. Part of the background research on the architectural history of Singapore for this essay was made possible by a grant (WBS No. R-295-000-127-112) from the National University of Singapore's Academic Research Fund.

2 Sandy Isenstadt, "Contested Contexts", in *Site Matters: Design Concepts, Histories, and Strategies*, ed. Carol J. Burns and Andrea Kahn (London: Routledge, 2005), p. 157.

3 莫玮玮, "我的父亲莫理光", 联合早报, 11 September 2013.

4 Such bookcases filled with translated masterpieces – many written by winners of the Nobel Prize in Literature – from a wide array of countries were commonly found in the homes of literary and aspiring literary figures in the developing world. See Amitav Ghosh, "The March of the Novel through History: The Testimony of My Grandfather's Bookcase", *The Kenyon Review*, vol. 20, no. 2, 1998, pp. 13–24.

FIG. 2 Members of the first council of the Society of Malayan Architects, established in 1958 to represent the Anglophone Chinese among Singapore's pioneer architects of the time. Standing (left to right): Robert Y. K. Yim, Wong Foo Nam, Ang Kheng Leng and Ho Kok Hoe. Sitting (left to right): K. C. Chung, Eu Jin Seow, Ng Keng Siang and Kee Yeap (Source: *Journal of the Society of Malayan Architects*, vol. 1, no. 1, 1958).

5 Chen Chong Swee, *Unfettered Ink: The Writings of Chen Chong Swee*, trans. Teck Seng Chow, Ngee Hui Goh and Kum Hoon Ng (Singapore: National Gallery Singapore, 2017); Marco C. F. Hsü, *A Brief History of Malayan Art*, trans. Lai Chee Kien (Singapore: Millennium Books, 1999).

6 Ho Weng Hin and Tan Kar Lin, "Ho Kwong Yew", in *Southeast Asian Personalities of Chinese Descent: A Biographical Dictionary*, ed. Leo Sury-adinata (Singapore: Institute of Southeast Asian Studies, 2012), pp. 338–40.

7 Eu Jin Seow's mother was a descendent of Tan Tock Seng, one of the wealthiest revenue farmers and philanthropists in the early 19th-century Straits Settlements, and his father was a general manager at the Ho Hong Bank, one of the oldest of the local banks that merged to become the Overseas-Chinese Banking Corporation in the 1930s. For the life of Eu, see his interview with the Oral History Centre, National Archives of Singapore, 4 January 1980, available at https://nas.gov.sg. Lim Chong Keat's uncle was Sir Lim Han Hoe, a physician and politician who was the second Malayan to be knighted, and his brother is Lim Chong Eu, a former chief minister

of Penang. For the life of Lim, see Jiat-Hwee Chang, "On Pioneer Malayan Architect Lim Chong Keat", 4 March 2015, available at https://blog.nus.edu.sg. Victor Chew's grandfather was Chew Boon Lay, an industrialist and plantation owner in the late 19th and early 20th centuries. Chew is also a relative of Khoo Teck Puat, a banker, hotelier and, at one point in the second half of the 20th century, the wealthiest man in Singapore. See Hoong Bee Lok, "Victor Chew: An Architect" (B. Arch. Elective Study, National University of Singapore, 1981). For the life of Lee, see Joanna H. S. Tan, "Lee Kip Lin", in *Singapore Infopedia*, available at https://eresources.nlb.gov.sg.

8 Ai Lin Chua, "Imperial Subjects, Straits Citizens: Anglophone Asians and the Struggle for Political Rights in Inter-War Singapore", in *Paths Not Taken: Political Pluralism in Post-War Singapore*, ed. Carl A. Trocki and Michael D. Barr (Singapore: NUS Press, 2008).

9 Personal correspondence with Mok Wei Wei about William S. W. Lim. For Alfred Wong, see Alfred Hong Kwok Wong, *Recollections of Life in an Accidental Nation* (Singapore: Select Books, 2016).

were with both Western art theories and avant-garde art practices, and, more impressively, their ability to situate the region's art within this broader discourse.[5] The same could be said in relation to the realm of architecture. It was Ho Kwong Yew (1903–1942) – a bilingual architect, art collector and good friend of the prominent Chinese artist Xu Beihong – who was creating the most imaginative and daring modern architecture in Singapore during the 1930s, a time when most Singapore-based European architects were still dressing buildings built with modern materials and technologies in either antiquated Neoclassical garb or an imitative Art Deco style.[6] Although the younger Mok practised in a later time and context, his architectural sensibility should be seen in this lineage of Chinese cosmopolitanism in Singapore.

Mok graduated from the School of Architecture at the National University of Singapore in 1982, around 25 years after the pioneering generation of Singaporean architects returned from their architectural education in Britain, Australia and the United States. Among them were key figures such as Eu Jin Seow (1920–1993), FIG. 2 Lim Chong Keat (b. 1930), Victor Chew (b. 1928) and Lee Kip Lin (1925–2011), all of whom were descendants of prominent Straits Chinese families, a section of society belonging firmly to the Anglophone-Chinese community that had constituted the colonial socio-economic elite.[7] They spoke English, Malay and a smattering of their own Chinese dialects. Culturally, they were cosmopolitan figures, but were primarily oriented to the West and to the hybrid Peranakan culture of the region.[8] Two architects in particular – William S. W. Lim (b. 1932), who was later Mok's mentor, and Alfred Wong (b. 1930) – received some level of Chinese education in their youth but they are largely Anglophone and, to my knowledge, do not speak Mandarin fluently or write in Chinese.[9] Another group of locally trained pioneer architects, who joined the profession in the early 1960s, were likewise exemplified by figures from Peranakan families, including Tay Kheng Soon (b. 1940) and Wee Chwee Heng (b. 1940). Although from middle-class rather than leading Straits Chinese families, both were Anglophone Chinese like their predecessors, and studied at elite English-language schools such as Anglo-Chinese School and Raffles Institution.

The Anglophone architects were the key protagonists behind the construction of a post-independence architecture for Singapore, which they called "Malayan Architecture". This was part of a larger cultural movement in the 1950s and 1960s that aspired to create different art forms – from literature to painting, from theatre to architecture – for a multicultural and multi-ethnic independent Malaya, which then included Singapore. Many of the pioneer architects equated Malayan Architecture to Tropical Modernism for at least two reasons. Firstly, Tropical Architecture was an international discourse that was hugely influential in the mid-twentieth century, and many pioneer architects were taught it during their architectural education.[10] Secondly, the abstract forms of modern architecture, and the privileging of climatic conditions as the modifier of such forms, allowed the pioneer architects to avoid any overt cultural references in their architecture, particularly references associated with any ethnic groups in Malaya. As the decolonizing years in Malaya were rife with inter-ethnic tensions, mainly as a result of the legacy of colonial racialization, it was important for the pioneer architects to suppress any reference to cultural motifs or symbols associated with any ethnic group, particularly the economically dominant Chinese.[11] After Singapore broke away from Malaysia in 1965, the marginal Chinese culture would be further marginalized, as English soon became the lingua franca. This led to the end of Chinese-language schools in 1983, after years of falling enrolment. In 1980, Nanyang University – once the only Chinese-language tertiary institution outside of Greater China – was subsumed into the University of Singapore to form the National University of Singapore (NUS). [FIG. 3]

It was in the midst of this period that Mok entered architecture school in 1977. Along with a few of his classmates, notably Tan Kay Ngee and Ho Puay Peng, [FIG. 4] Mok was part of a group of students who had to transition between Chinese-language schools, where they had received their education until senior high school or pre-university level, and the English-language education at NUS. Being well-versed in Chinese literary and cultural traditions while also excelling in their English-language architectural education at both local and overseas schools, Mok and his classmates were probably the first group of truly bilingual and bicultural architects in post-independence Singapore.[12] Unlike his predecessors and peers who were solely educated in English-language schools, Mok was – and still is – perhaps able to tap into a different cultural sensibility, with its attendant visual and spatial imaginaries. At various points in his career, when the right opportunities have arisen thanks to an appropriate programme, site or brief, Mok has been able to express his and his clients' Chinese-ness in a spatial manner that reflects his multiculturalism and cosmopolitanism, as well as the global milieu in which he operates.

FIG. 3 The original Nantah Arch – the first entrance to Nanyang University in 1955 – at old Upper Jurong Road, today's Jurong West Street 93, c. 2000.

FIG. 4 Mok (second from the left) with (left to right) his former classmate Ho Puay Peng, the Chinese architect Chang Yung Ho and another old classmate, Tan Kay Ngee, in 2017.

10 See Jiat-Hwee Chang, *A Genealogy of Tropical Architecture: Colonial Networks, Nature and Technoscience* (London: Routledge, 2016).

11 I have written about this elsewhere. See "Race and Tropical Architecture: The Climate of Decolonization and Malayanization", in *Race and Modern Architecture*, ed. Irene Cheng, Charles L. Davis and Mabel O. Wilson (Pittsburgh: University of Pittsburgh Press, forthcoming).

12 Mok studied at Anglican High while Tan and Ho studied at Catholic High and Maris Stella High respectively. All three were Chinese-language missionary schools. Tan is an architect who also contributes frequently to Chinese newspapers and magazines in Singapore, Taiwan and Hong Kong. Ho is an architect as well as an art and architectural historian specializing in East Asia. Both Tan and Ho did not complete their architectural education in Singapore; they left to study at the Architectural Association (AA), London, and the University of Edinburgh respectively. While Mok's thesis project was selected as one of the best in his cohort, Tan's project at the AA won the 1985 RIBA International Competition for students.

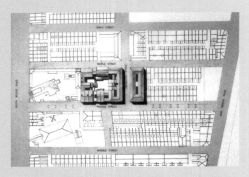

FIG. 5 The site plan of Chinatown Infill (1981–82), Mok's thesis project for Kreta Ayer district.

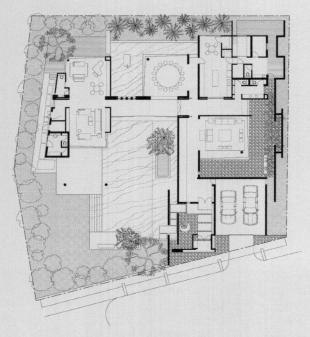

FIG. 6 The ground-floor plan of Morley Road House (1996–99).

13 See Mok Wei Wei (ed.), *Chinese More or Less: Mok Wei Wei + W Architects Singapore* (Berlin: Aedes Architecture Forum, 2006).

14 Ibid., unpaginated.

15 Fumihiko Maki, "Stillness and Plenitude: The Architecture of Yoshio Taniguchi", in *The Architecture of Yoshio Taniguchi*, ed. Yoshio Taniguchi (New York: Harry N. Abrams, 1999).

16 For a compelling reading of Pei's thesis project, see Henry Cobb's lecture delivered on 30 March 2017 at Harvard GSD, available at https://www.youtube.com/watch?v=zl7c5hqSQI4.

By drawing on this different cultural wellspring of ideas and imaginaries, cultivated by his deep immersion in the Chinese cosmopolitan environment of his upbringing and education, Mok has also been able to move away from – and explore alternatives to – the climatic-aesthetic dictates of Tropical Modernism that preoccupied the pioneer architects in Singapore.[13]

The Architectural Context of Situated Postmodernism

After graduating from NUS at the beginning of 1982, Mok was invited by William Lim to join his eponymous firm. Lim had been impressed by Mok's thesis project, Chinatown Infill (1981–82), which proposed an infill for the middle of Kreta Ayer district, the traditional heart of Singapore's Chinatown. FIG. 5 The project drew on Mok's deep reserve of Chinese cultural knowledge and imaginings, particularly those of the classical gardens of Suzhou. The sequential spatial experiences he carefully orchestrated in his design – those of revealing and concealing views, of expansion and contraction of spaces, and of centripetal and centrifugal movements – came from his multiple readings of Cao Xueqin's *The Story of the Stone*, one of the four great Chinese classical novels.[14] Although very much based on a Chinese cultural sensibility, the spatial conception in Mok's project is also very modern and thus transcultural in some ways. I have in mind here the architecture of Yoshio Taniguchi, especially when seen in relation to Mok's subsequent works inspired by Chinese spatial concepts, particularly Morley Road House (1996–99). FIG. 6 The Japanese architect combines the spatial qualities associated with two oppositional modernist archetypes – the court and the pavilion – by incorporating in a single building both stillness and dynamism, introverted and extroverted spaces, and centripetal and centrifugal movements.[15] I also think of Chinese-American architect Ieoh Ming Pei's thesis project at the Harvard Graduate School of Design (GSD) and his late works – specifically the Miho Museum (1997) and Suzhou Museum (2006) – that combine the spatial and formal vocabulary of modern architecture with Chinese aesthetic and spatial concepts.[16]

A point of clarification is perhaps needed here about Modernism, which is not a monolithic entity. The Modernism in Mok's thesis project is very different from the "High Modernism" adopted by the Singapore state and its agencies in urban planning and architectural design — the Urban Redevelopment Authority, the Housing and Development Board and the Public Works Department.[17] It is also distinct from the "Heroic Modernism" evident in 1970s projects by the city-state's pioneer architects, such as the Pearl Bank Apartments (1976), [FIG. 7] People's Park Complex (1973) [FIG. 8] and Woh Hup Complex (1973; today's Golden Mile Complex).[18] [FIG. 9] The High Modernism adopted by the Singapore state was very much a tabula rasa approach to historical urban fabric that involved the demolition of old buildings on a site, turning it into a blank slate for new and typically large-scale developments. Mok's Modernism, on the other hand, is a contextual one that is sensitive to what is already at the site, selectively conserving parts of an old building while modifying others. I consider it Modernist because it has a long tradition that can be traced back to what the Scottish polymath town planner Patrick Geddes called "conservative surgery" in the late nineteenth century. However, as this attitude to urban intervention was relegated to the sidelines and largely forgotten during the High Modernist period of the 1980s, many – including Mok himself – associated the approach with Postmodernism instead.

Mok's affinity with Postmodernism was also due to the influence of his mentor, William Lim. [FIG. 10] In the earlier phases of his career, Lim co-designed a few of Singapore's seminal modern buildings. These include the Singapore Conference Hall and Trade Union House (1965) when he was with the Malayan Architects Co-Partnership, and the Woh Hup Complex (1973) and the People's Park Complex (1973) when he was with Design Partnership. However, Lim began to be disenchanted with Modernism from around 1975. Among other things, he felt that the globally prevailing form of Modernism was leading to the destruction of traditional environments, the homogenizing of diverse place cultures and the alienation of humans from the built environment.[19] Lim began experimenting with Postmodernism from the late 1970s and, by the time he left DP Architects (which was the name Design Partnership took on after Tay Kheng Soon departed the firm in 1975) to establish William Lim Associates (WLA) in 1981, he was highly sympathetic to Postmodernist perspectives on architecture.

One of the first projects that Mok worked on upon joining WLA sought to redress some of these oversights of Modernism. Bu Ye Tian (1982) was a proposal to conserve two rows of shophouses at

17 For High Modernism, see James C. Scott, *Seeing Like a State: How Certain Schemes to Improve the Human Condition Have Failed* (New Haven: Yale University Press, 1998).

18 I prefer to use "Heroic" over "Brutalist" to describe these 1970s buildings in Singapore. My use of "Heroic" draws from Mark Pasnik, Michael Kubo and Chris Grimley (eds.), *Heroic: Concrete Architecture and the New Boston* (New York: The Monacelli Press, 2015).

19 William S. W. Lim, *Cities for the People: Reflections of a Southeast Asian Architect* (Singapore: Select Books, 1990). See, in particular, chapters 1, 3 and 5.

FIG. 7 Pearl Bank Apartments (1976), designed by Tan Cheng Siong, Archurban Architects Planners.

FIG. 8 People's Park Complex (1973), designed by William Lim, Tay Kheng Soon and Koh Seow Chuan, Design Partnership.

FIG. 9 Woh Hup Complex (1973), designed by William Lim, Tay Kheng Soon and Gan Eng Oon, Design Partnership.

FIG. 10 Mok with his mentor William Lim, c. 1990s.

FIG. 11 An artist's impression of Bu Ye Tian (1982), a proposal by William Lim, Dr Goh Poh Seng and others. Mok was one of the main architects behind the project.

FIG. 12 A portrait of Dr Goh Poh Seng, c. 1970s.

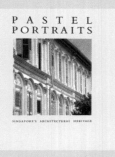

FIG. 13 *Pastel Portraits: Singapore's Architectural Heritage*, 1984.

20 M. Gretchen, "Boat Quay's Business-man and Poet", *Straits Times*, 6 May 1983; M. Gretchen, "New Face Plan for Boat Quay", *Straits Times*, 6 May 1983; Katherine Ong, "Plan for Tourist Town at Boat Quay", *Singapore Monitor*, 5 May 1983.

21 Carl G. Larson, "Adaptive Reuse: Singapore River", in *Mimar 12: Architecture in Development*, ed. Hasan-Uddin Khan (Singapore: Concept Media, 1984), pp. 32–39.

22 A newspaper advertisement listed its name as "Seminar on adaptive reuse: integrating traditional areas into the modern urban fabric", stating that it was a joint programme of Harvard University and the Massachusetts Institute of Technology. See *Business Times*, 14 April 1984.

Boat Quay. FIG. 11 The project was led by local playwright and poet Dr Goh Poh Seng FIG. 12 and a group of "prominent private sector figures", including Lim and individuals from the banking, telecommunications and tourism sectors. At that time, the state was planning to resettle inhabitants of these old and dilapidated shophouses, and the properties seemed destined – like many others before them – to be demolished. The group wanted to conserve the buildings and, more importantly, the social and cultural histories and memories associated with them. Between July and November 1982, it came up with a proposal to turn the area into a commercially feasible cultural centre, which consisted of artists' studios, workshops for traditional craftspeople, an art gallery, premises for clan associations, a *wayang* (traditional Chinese opera) court, restaurants, a Chinese tea house, a Chinese inn with luxuriously furnished rooms and a classical Chinese garden.[20] Mok, who was one of the main architects behind the project, deployed a set of design strategies for Bu Ye Tian that were similar to his thesis project. He proposed demolishing some portions of the buildings in order to reconfigure the back lanes and introduce internal courtyards between the two back-facing rows of shophouses.[21]

The idea of renovating and retrofitting historical buildings and reprogramming them with more commercially relevant uses was not a new one at the time. The group referred to international precedents such as San Francisco's Fisherman's Wharf, London's Covent Garden and Sydney's The Rocks. However, the proposal was seminal in the history of the conservation of built heritage in Singapore. Following its public presentation on 6 May 1983, Bu Ye Tian was reported on the front pages of the city-state's major newspapers. Although not realized, the proposal changed public perceptions towards the derelict shophouses, which were previously viewed as slums to be cleared. The Singapore government and its agencies also started to view conservation and adaptive reuse of shophouses more favourably. The day after the media reported on the proposal, a public competition for ideas on how to preserve and revitalize Boat Quay was announced by the state planning agency, the Urban Redevelopment Authority (URA), and the non-government organization, the Singapore Institute of Planners. Later in 1983, Lim was appointed to chair a Singapore Coordinating Committee to plan an international seminar on the adaptive reuse of old buildings, which took place from 28 April to 2 May 1984.[22] The committee also published *Pastel Portraits*, a book documenting the historical buildings and districts of Singapore. FIG. 13 In his foreword, S. Rajaratnam, then Singapore's

Second Deputy Prime Minister, endorsed the need to conserve shophouses as a record of the history of Singapore.[23] This marked a shift in the official policy towards the shophouses, and the URA followed up by completing its first conservation programme of Tanjong Pagar shophouses in 1987, while the first conservation master plan that included different shophouse districts was announced in 1989.

Bu Ye Tian could only be successfully pulled off by a multidisciplinary team with not just design skills but also commercial and policy nous. As Mok noted, Lim is a "big-picture man", especially adept at comprehending social and economic statistics, and finding creative planning and design strategies to work within these constraints. Besides his early training in urban planning at GSD, Lim also had a long involvement in urban activism through, for instance, the Singapore Planning and Urban Research Group (SPUR), which existed from 1966 to 1975. [FIG. 14] Furthermore, Lim was a "great convener" who was, and probably still is, very well connected to both the local and international intelligentsia.[24] The collaboration in Bu Ye Tian happened partly because of his friendship with Dr Goh, which could be traced to the 1960s, when Lim was on the editorial board of *Tumasek*, the literary journal founded by the poet. Mok acknowledged that working closely with Lim during this period taught him to combine his own interest in the meticulous crafting of architecture with broader perspectives. Later in his career, Mok played an important role in shaping larger policies pertaining to heritage conservation and urban planning by serving as a board member on various government agencies and statutory boards, such as the Preservation of Sites and Monuments (previously known as the Preservation of Monuments Board) (1999–2016), the Urban Redevelopment Authority (2006–18), the Singapore Land Authority (since 2015) and the Jurong Town Corporation (since 2019).

If Bu Ye Tian represents an episode in which Mok benefitted from Lim's extensive local network and developed his own interest in heritage conservation and rejuvenation, the trip the duo took to the United States and Japan in 1983 signifies an occasion on which he was exposed to his mentor's international connections, encouraging his interest in Postmodernism. During that trip, the pair visited a number of early Postmodernist buildings in the United States, such as the Portland Building (1982) by Michael Graves and New York's AT&T Building (1984) by Philip Johnson and John Burgee. What impressed them most, however, were the works of Frank Gehry, a former classmate of Lim at Harvard. [FIG. 15] Gehry drove them around in Los Angeles and showed them a

FIG. 14 A 1967 publication by Singapore Planning and Urban Research Group.

FIG. 15 William Lim and Frank Gehry, Singapore, 2015

23 S. Rajaratnam, "Foreword", in *Pastel Portraits: Singapore's Architectural Heritage*, ed. Gretchen Liu (Singapore: Singapore Coordinating Committee, 1984), p. 4.

24 "The great convener" is how architect Tay describes Lim. See Tay Kheng Soon, "On William Lim", in *Nolimits: Articulating William Lim*, ed. William S. W. Lim et al. (Singapore: Select Publishing, 2002).

FIG. 16 Church of Our Saviour (1985–87).

FIG. 17 Tampines North Community Centre (1986–89), with further extensions (1990–92).

25 Benjamin Forgey, "Frank Gehry's Eye for L.A.", *Washington Post*, 2 May 1987.

number of his recently completed buildings. These works from the late 1970s and early 1980s are rather different from his celebrated later works. Before Gehry completed the Vitra Design Museum at Weil am Rhein in 1989 and then adopted software originally designed for the aeronautical industry to produce widely celebrated icons such as the Guggenheim Bilbao (1997) and the Walt Disney Concert Hall, Los Angeles (2003), he was known more for a fragmented collage approach to design. Despite its idiosyncrasies, this was in fact very contextual in that it emerged out of Gehry's responses to the peculiar urbanism of the Los Angeles metropolitan area.[25] Not only were the formal and spatial qualities of such early works unusual, the building materials used for these projects were also unconventional. Gehry often used cheap, quotidian materials such as chain-link fences, corrugated steel sheets and timber studs, and left them exposed on his buildings. These materials were readily seen in the urban sprawl of Los Angeles, but more significantly, they were practical solutions for an architect working on projects with low budgets.

These aspects of Gehry's architecture would prove to be instructive for and influential on Mok's design approach, especially after Singapore was hit by its first economic recession in the post-independence era in 1985. This affected both the construction industry and the architecture profession, and a boutique architectural firm such as WLA survived mainly on small addition-and-alteration projects. One of the largest was the Church of Our Saviour (1985–87). Following a trend at that time, the congregation had bought an old cinema – the Venus Theatre, completed and opened in 1965 – to convert into their church. Mok's design took references from the original language of the cinema, for example by keeping and accentuating the mosaic patterns. This move to retain some of the original structure and finishes was not just contextual, but also practical because of the low budget. In a way, the now demolished design was an extension of Mok's interest in keeping and strategically modifying existing buildings, evolved from his thesis and the Bu Ye Tian proposal. But the design, with its juxtaposition of different geometric shapes in bright colours in a manner akin to the designs of the Italian Memphis Group, was obviously also influenced by what Mok had seen of Gehry's works and by Lim's playful attitude towards architectural form. FIG. 16 However, the project that bears the greatest imprint of Gehry's influence was probably a new-build: the Tampines North Community Centre (1986–89). Here, the building was fragmented into individual programmatic elements that were articulated as discrete volumes and loosely arranged within a rectilinear frame. FIG. 17

The Socio-Economic Context of Revaluing Design

After this initial phase of experimenting with Postmodernist architecture, Mok became "tired of the exuberance" associated with it. From the 1990s, he changed path to produce a body of works that is more familiarly modern. This decade would also see WLA evolve from boutique design, gaining two new types of commissions: condominiums and high-profile public buildings. The Paterson Edge (1996–99) was the firm's first completed condominium project, and also the developer SembCorp Properties' maiden residential project. Key to the project being awarded to WLA was Leong Weng Chee, then the developer's general manager, who had been Mok's senior at the NUS School of Architecture and later went to Harvard to obtain a Master's in Design Studies specializing in finance, law and real estate. FIG. 18 With his unusual background in both architecture and real estate, Leong was able to see the commercial value of good design.

As The Paterson Edge sits on a thin sliver of land too narrow for standard condominium design, the developer was willing to try an unconventional design targeting a niche market. That was perhaps why Mok, known at that time for designing exquisite interiors and houses, was given the commission. In approaching the project, Mok did a few things. First, he requested a waiver of the standard 5-metre (16½-foot) setback requirement from the planning authorities. Once waived, Mok then introduced the glass curtain wall, which till then had never been used for a residential project in Singapore. This choice of facade ensured that the small units in the development would be visually connected to the outside and not feel claustrophobic. FIG. 19 The glass curtain wall was carefully detailed as a thin elegant "skin" that appears to peel away at the edges. Mok also put the swimming pool requisite for any condominium development on the roof to create a sense of openness. Here again, he detailed the pool to have an infinity edge on one of the long sides, and then enclosed one of the short sides with a laminated glass wall to accentuate the illusion of a boundless space. FIG. 20

The architectural aesthetic of The Paterson Edge was conceived to complement the marketing concept of "urban living". Applied to a development that consists of relatively small two- and three-bedroom apartments, the aesthetic could be interpreted as one that helped to blur the thresholds between the home and the city, thus enabling the residents to immerse themselves in the excitement of living in the city centre. This novel concept proved to be very successful commercially.

FIG. 18 Leong Weng Chee, c. 1990s.

FIG. 19 Interior view of an apartment at The Paterson Edge (1996–99).

FIG. 20 View of the rooftop swimming pool at The Paterson Edge.

FIG. 21 Mok on stage to receive the President's Design Award Designer of the Year 2007 from President S. R. Nathan.

26 Diana Oon, "Projects Not Selling? Is Your Pricing Right?", *Business Times*, 2 October 1997, p. 4.

27 Jeremy Au Yong, "Glass House Living a Clear Winner: Residents Rave About Lush Views, Brushing Aside Privacy and Heat Issues", *Straits Times*, 10 October 2004; Michelle Ho, "Lap of Luxury", ibid., 3 November 2002.

28 Arthur Sim, "Return of the Condo Heroes", ibid., 17 June 2001.

29 Ministry of Information and The Arts, *Renaissance City Report: Culture and the Arts in Renaissance Singapore* (Singapore: Ministry of Information and The Arts, 2000).

Despite the advent of the Asian Financial Crisis in the middle of 1997, the project sold out five days after its official launch in September that year.[26] This started the design trend of condominiums in Singapore having glass curtain-wall facades and rooftop swimming pools.[27] It also initiated a tendency in real-estate marketing to emphasize design and other less tangible values, which led to other design-centric boutique firms such as SCDA Architects and WOHA being commissioned to design condominiums targeting niche markets.[28] In the subsequent years, WLA and its successor firm W Architects (WA) – formed after Lim retired in 2003 – took on more condominium projects of a similar nature. Another notable early example for WLA was The Loft (1996–2002), which also came about because the developer, Pidemco Land (the predecessor of CapitaLand), had an architecture-trained employee, Poon Hin Kong, who recognized the value of good design. Over the years, CapitaLand and Simon Cheong's SCGlobal, which specializes in developing luxurious residential properties, have commissioned WA to work on a series of such niche-market developments.

The emergence of design-conscious property developments in Singapore coincided with a larger revaluation of arts and culture in general, and design in particular, in the city-state. Two state-led reforms at the turn of the millennium were indicative of this. First, the 1989 Report of the Advisory Council on Culture and the Arts provided a comprehensive slate of recommendations intended to turn Singapore into a culturally vibrant society. This led to the establishments of arts and cultural institutions such as the Singapore Art Museum, Asian Civilisations Museum and Esplanade – Theatres on the Bay. The 1989 report was expanded upon by the second and third Renaissance City Plans of 2000 and 2008.[29] By then, the ambition was to establish Singapore as a global arts city and cultural centre, thereby creating an environment conducive to creative and knowledge-based industries. The economic rationality of cultural development was closely linked to a second state-led reform taking place at around the same time. In response to the Asian Financial Crisis and the bursting of the global dot-com bubble, which led to the contraction of Singapore's economy, an Economic Review Committee was appointed by the government in 2001 to make recommendations on restructuring the city-state's economy. It identified the creative industry, involving art, design and media, as one of the three new sectors of growth for Singapore. One of the outcomes was the establishment of a new national agency for promoting design, the DesignSingapore Council. This agency set up the President's Design Award in 2006 to elevate the status of Singaporean design, and Mok was the recipient of its Designer of the Year award the following year.[30] FIG. 21

Economic restructuring in Singapore also led to Mok and other similar private-sector designers being asked to design public buildings. This was the result of what some have called a neoliberal economic policy and the privatization of certain public assets and services. In the 1990s, as part of the government's effort to "devolve the non-policy and non-regulatory functions from its various ministries and departments", the state's main architecture service provider, the Public Works Department (PWD), was corporatized.[31] Likewise the Technical Services Group of Jurong Town Corporation and the Building and Development Division of the Housing and Development Board were corporatized in 2001 and 2003 respectively. This conversion of former government entities into private companies opened up public-sector projects to private architectural firms. This emphasis on design excellence as one of the main criteria of evaluation for important public institutional buildings helped ensure that Mok and his firm won commissions to design important state buildings such as the National Museum of Singapore (2002–6) FIG. 22 and Victoria Theatre and Victoria Concert Hall (2009–14). FIG. 23

Like other socio-economic transformations, economic restructuring was also mediated through people. The outcomes of these transformations thus depended on the judgements and actions of individuals. Just as Mok was presented the opportunities to introduce new architectural concepts to condominiums because managerial-level employees working for large developers saw value in his design, the same could be said for his involvement in the design of public buildings. This was especially so for Mok's first major cultural institution: the extension and redevelopment of the National Museum of Singapore. WLA was originally engaged to act as interior design consultants, with the newly corporatized PWD as the appointed architects. Lee Chor Lin, who was then the director of the museum, FIG. 24 appreciated Mok's design inputs and enlarged his involvement by giving him architectural-design responsibilities and appointing the firm as design consultants.

FIG. 22 National Museum of Singapore, after its extension and redevelopment by Mok (2002–6).

FIG. 23 Victoria Theatre and Victoria Concert Hall, after its conservation and redevelopment by Mok (2009–14).

FIG. 24 Lee Chor Lin, c. 2012.

FIG. 25 Ng Weng Pan (left) and Mok Wei Wei, c. 2012.

30 Justin Zhuang, Dawn Lim and Sheere Ng (eds.), *Fifty Years of Singapore Design* (Singapore: DesignSingapore Council, 2015).

31 "Formation of PWD Corporation (PWD Co) and the Building and Construction Authority (BCA)", press release by the Ministry of National Development, 2 October 1998, available at https://www.bca.gov.sg/newsroom/others/pr021098_mnd.pdf.

This essay has been about contexts, specifically the different forms of contexts that shaped and informed Mok's architecture. Contexts, however, do not exist without people, people who interpret, mediate, address and even transform the very contexts they encounter. The relationship between context and people is perhaps akin to that between structure and agency in historical research. By way of selected episodes in Mok's life and career, we have seen how he exercised his agency through his architectural designs. Architectural agency, however, is collaborative in nature. Foregrounded in this narrative were the roles played by Mok's nurturing father who cultivated his talent; the mentoring figure of Lim who exposed Mok to broader architectural and planning perspectives; and the various enlightened managerial figures who recognized Mok's ability and entrusted him with major commissions. Besides them, the most important people in realizing Mok's architecture are the people in his firm who worked alongside him and assisted in realizing the architectural designs documented in this monograph. Among them, Ng Weng Pan, who joined the firm in 1989 and became Mok's partner after William Lim retired, is particularly important. FIG. 25 Although there are too many other names to mention in this essay, I imagine they must have left their marks behind in the firm's beautifully conceived and meticulously executed designs.

References

Au Yong, Jeremy, "Glass House Living a Clear Winner: Residents Rave About Lush Views, Brushing Aside Privacy and Heat Issues", *Straits Times*, 10 October 2004.

Chang, Jiat-Hwee, *A Genealogy of Tropical Architecture: Colonial Networks, Nature and Technoscience*, London: Routledge, 2016.

———, "Race and Tropical Architecture: The Climate of Decolonization and Malayanization", in *Race and Modern Architecture*, edited by Irene Cheng, Charles L. Davis and Mabel O. Wilson, Pittsburgh: University of Pittsburgh Press, forthcoming.

Chen, Chong Swee, *Unfettered Ink: The Writings of Chen Chong Swee*, translated by Teck Seng Chow, Ngee Hui Goh and Kum Hoon Ng, Singapore: National Gallery Singapore, 2017.

Chua, Ai Lin, "Imperial Subjects, Straits Citizens: Anglophone Asians and the Struggle for Political Rights in Inter-War Singapore", in *Paths Not Taken: Political Pluralism in Post-War Singapore*, edited by Carl A. Trocki and Michael D. Barr, Singapore: NUS Press, 2008.

Forgey, Benjamin, "Frank Gehry's Eye for L.A.", *Washington Post*, 2 May 1987.

Ghosh, Amitav, "The March of the Novel through History: The Testimony of My Grandfather's Bookcase", *The Kenyon Review*, vol. 20, no. 2, 1998, pp. 13–24.

Gretchen, M., "Boat Quay's Businessman and Poet", *Straits Times*, 6 May 1983.

———, "New Face Plan for Boat Quay", *Straits Times*, 6 May 1983.

Ho, Michelle, "Lap of Luxury", *Straits Times*, 3 November 2002.

Ho, Weng Hin, and Kar Lin Tan, "Ho Kwong Yew", in *Southeast Asian Personalities of Chinese Descent: A Biographical Dictionary*, edited by Leo Suryadinata, Singapore: Institute of Southeast Asian Studies, 2012, pp. 338–40.

Hoong, Bee Lok, "Victor Chew: An Architect", B. Arch. Elective Study, National University of Singapore, 1981.

Hsü, Marco C. F., *A Brief History of Malayan Art*, translated by Chee Kien Lai, Singapore: Millennium Books, 1999.

Isenstadt, Sandy, "Contested Contexts", in *Site Matters: Design Concepts, Histories, and Strategies*, edited by Carol J. Burns and Andrea Kahn, London: Routledge, 2005, pp. 157–83.

Larson, Carl G., "Adaptive Reuse: Singapore River", in *Mimar 12: Architecture in Development*, edited by Hasan-Uddin Khan, Singapore: Concept Media, 1984, pp. 32–39.

Lim, William S. W., *Cities for the People: Reflections of a Southeast Asian Architect*, Singapore: Select Books, 1990.

Maki, Fumihiko, "Stillness and Plenitude: The Architecture of Yoshio Taniguchi", in *The Architecture of Yoshio Taniguchi*, edited by Yoshio Taniguchi, New York: Harry N. Abrams, 1999.

Ministry of Information and The Arts, *Renaissance City Report: Culture and the Arts in Renaissance Singapore*, Singapore: Ministry of Information and The Arts, 2000.

Mok, Wei Wei (ed.), *Chinese More or Less: Mok Wei Wei + W Architects Singapore*, Berlin: Aedes Architecture Forum, 2006.

Ong, Katherine, "Plan for Tourist Town at Boat Quay", *Singapore Monitor*, 5 May 1983.

Oon, Diana, "Projects Not Selling? Is Your Pricing Right?", *Business Times*, 2 October 1997, p. 4.

Pasnik, Mark, Michael Kubo and Chris Grimley (eds.), *Heroic: Concrete Architecture and the New Boston*, New York: The Monacelli Press, 2015.

Scott, James C., *Seeing Like a State: How Certain Schemes to Improve the Human Condition Have Failed*, New Haven: Yale University Press, 1998.

Sim, Arthur, "Return of the Condo Heroes", *Straits Times*, 17 June 2001.

Tay, Kheng Soon, "On William Lim", in *Nolimits: Articulating William Lim*, edited by William S. W. Lim, Robert Powell, Teng Wui Leong, Kah Wee Lee, Lena U Wen Lim, Kah Heng Tan, Kim Nam Chow and Jon Kher Kaw, Singapore: Select Publishing, 2002.

Wong, Alfred Hong Kwok, *Recollections of Life in an Accidental Nation*, Singapore: Select Books, 2016.

Zhuang, Justin, Dawn Lim and Sheere Ng (eds.), *Fifty Years of Singapore Design*, Singapore: DesignSingapore Council, 2015.

莫玮玮，"我的父亲莫理光"，
联合早报, 11 September 2013.

01

REFRACT

IN SEARCH OF
FUNDAMENTALS

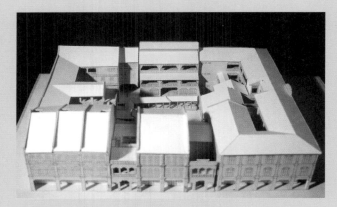

FIG. 1 A model of the Chinatown Infill thesis project (1981–82).

FIG. 2 Boat Quay in the early 1980s.

1 My thesis project tutor, Dr Pinna Indorf, encouraged me to take this approach as she was passionate about Asian and Southeast-Asian cultures, having researched historic Hindu and Buddhist architecture in the region. The American architect was an inspiring design critic who taught at the NUS School of Architecture from 1977 to 2002. Prior to that, she practised in Bangkok with Dr Sumet Jumsai from 1968 to 1974.

My architectural journey began in the era of Postmodernism. Upon graduating from architecture school in 1982, I joined the eponymous firm of the pioneer Singapore architect William S. W. Lim, who had been one of the foremost proponents of Postmodernism in the city-state since the late 1970s.

My graduation thesis, Chinatown Infill (1981–82), together with two other projects I undertook fresh out of school – Bu Ye Tian (1982) and Goh's House (1982–84) – were heritage and conservation works that reflected Postmodernism's advocacy of using local histories as a counterpoint to the faceless International Style that had been proliferating across the world. My choice to conserve shophouses in Singapore's Chinatown for my thesis was largely influenced by the extensive coverage of conservation projects in magazines and publications of the time, especially those from the United States. This was where the term "adaptive reuse" was coined to describe the repurposing of historic buildings.

Chinatown Infill also formalized a spatial culture that had been embedded within me – that of a Chinese garden. This had emerged in my struggle to incorporate more cultural content to a central space in the project's site, enabling it to become the focal point of the larger conservation area.[1] I created this by reorganizing the service blocks and the back lanes behind the conserved shophouses. Using elements such as a roofed corridor (長廊) and a pavilion, I managed to not only create a transition of scale from the surrounding three-storey shophouses but also infuse a picturesque quality in the tiny courtyard space. FIG. 1 The idea of a "Chinese garden" was reinforced by celebrating the various approaches from the streets to the courtyard, offering a journey of discovery through spaces that conceal and reveal.

Up till then, as a Singaporean Chinese living in Southeast Asia, I had neither been to China nor visited an authentic Chinese garden. The vivid image of a Chinese garden with all its spatial characteristics, and the ease with which I employed them, must have come from years of reading classical Chinese texts while growing up, as well as seeing pictures of these gardens in books and paintings. Like many overseas Chinese, I also regularly consumed popular period dramas produced in Hong Kong and China, which were often set in Chinese gardens. This spatial typology would emerge time and again in the office's works over the decades.

Soon after joining William Lim Associates, my thesis found its way into practical application. Lim, who is very much an urban activist, was then advocating the conservation of the historic quarters of Singapore, beyond the preservation of individual monuments. He initiated Bu Ye Tian[2] with the late Dr Goh Poh Seng, a respected local playwright and poet, to conserve two rows of shophouses which had been slated for demolition. FIG. 2 Situated near the mouth of the Singapore River where Stamford Raffles, the British founder of modern Singapore, had landed, this prominent conservation project would transform the riverfront into a vibrant destination with activities in the day and night. Being tasked to design the project, I had the opportunity to apply concepts from my thesis. As the two rows of back-to-back shophouses had back lanes that were completely taken over by various extensions over the years, I proposed recovering them to create a series of courtyards joined by an internal street, as well as giving an additional frontage to the river- and street-facing shophouses. While Bu Ye Tian was not accepted in full by the government, this ground-up initiative played a major role in accelerating the conservation movement in Singapore.

Around the same time, Dr Goh bought a shophouse in the historic Emerald Hill area, which was gazetted for conservation several years after. This was traditionally an enclave occupied by rich Peranakan families, and Dr Goh, who was himself a Peranakan, wanted this to be his family home.[3] The refurbishment of Goh's House became my first built project after graduation. When it was completed, Dr Goh, who admired Southeast-Asian culture, furnished it with crafts and materials from the region. FIG. 3 This was a refreshing ambience for me as I had grown up in an environment steeped in Chinese culture and tradition. It prompted my interest in collecting crafts and artefacts from the region, and I even used some of these in various of my interior works in the 1990s. FIG. 4 For over two decades, I've also tried to immerse myself in the material culture of Southeast Asia.

FIG. 3 Living room of Goh's House (1982–84).

FIG. 4 Sarawakian mats featured on the ceiling of Man & His Woman boutique (1990–91).

2 This can be loosely translated from Chinese to mean "a place of ceaseless activity". While "不夜天" was the traditional Chinese name of a different part of Chinatown known as Kreta Ayer in Malay, Dr Goh decided to use it for our proposal as it was not well known in modern Singapore.

3 Peranakan Chinese, or Straits-born Chinese, are the descendants of local Malays and Chinese immigrants who came to the Malay Archipelago – including areas that were later to become British Malaya (now Malaysia and Singapore), the Dutch East Indies (now Indonesia) and Southern Thailand – between the 15th and 17th centuries. Historically, the Peranakans were better assimilated into the local cultures, having adopted partially or in full customs of the Malay Archipelago. In Singapore, many were the elites of society, and were more loyal to the British than to China. Mostly educated in English and with the ability to speak two or more languages, Peranakans were usually traders who successfully acted as the middlemen among the British, Chinese and Malays. Many Peranakans have lived for generations along the Straits of Malacca.

FIG. 5 Tampines North Community Centre (1986–89).

FIG. 6 Church of Our Saviour (1985–87).

4 The original massing of the building is no longer recognizable, as the community centre was extended by another firm in the early 2000s.

Embracing Postmodernism

Besides the theoretical thrust of Postmodernism, I was also influenced by it as a style. With Lim, I completed two stylistically "PoMo" buildings: Church of Our Saviour (1985–87) and Tampines North Community Centre (1986–89). These were the results of an eye-opening and engaging trip Lim and I took to Los Angeles in 1983 to visit the architect Frank Gehry. The two men seemed to share a special bond as they were at Harvard at the same time, and both had left without completing their master degrees in town planning, thinking it was unnecessary in advancing their architectural careers. Gehry drove us around Downtown Los Angeles, pointing out quirky features that dotted the city, including a small plane perched on top of a house. We visited his early projects in the Venice Beach area, and dined in his home under the famous tumbling glass cube that presided above the dining table. Many years later, Gehry came to Singapore to give a lecture and invited Lim on stage for a conversation. To my surprise, Lim recounted to a packed audience how cannabis was passed around the table at the end of that dinner, and that the substance failed to elicit a response from me!

Nevertheless, Gehry's work had a great impact on me. I was struck by how contextual, and even vernacular, his seemingly outrageous architecture was. It was a language born out of his roots in Los Angeles and his love for avant-garde art. All the more remarkable is how the construction was always rational and economical in its means.

Tampines North Community Centre's fragmented massing owed its origins to Gehry's architecture, but I also introduced something that he perhaps would not have done: an ordering element in the form of a colonnade that held the fragments together. When seen from the exterior, this colonnade's regular rhythm appears as an extension of the orderly facade of the surrounding public-housing estate.[4] FIG. 5 This element of duality – regular versus irregular, orderliness versus playfulness, and the way the richness of a space is designed to be concealed and discovered – fascinates me till this day.

While the design approach for the Church of Our Saviour also displays the influence of Gehry, it was the culmination of a series of small house renovations that the office had been undertaking, as it then lacked bigger commissions. These refurbishment projects helped me to recognize the need to celebrate and incorporate the unique features of houses built in different eras, instead of erasing them for "improvement". This is an ethos I have pursued throughout my career. In our conversion of a 1960s cinema into this church, we not only kept the abundance of decorative motifs but even augmented them in the renovation. The result looks like a series of furniture designs by the Memphis Group strung together. FIG. 6 I remember thinking that this would complement the style of worship favoured by the church – it was part of the Charismatic movement and its services were always accompanied by a rock band on stage.[5]

Without these collaborations with Lim, I probably would not have embraced Postmodernism as a style so enthusiastically. Our projects in this era were very much the result of two very different personalities working together. Lim, being an extrovert, was naturally drawn towards the colourful language of Postmodernism, whereas I was an introvert who was by nature more contemplative and restrained. The layering of Tampines North Community Centre reflects this relationship, as it is preferable to read even a dynamic massing in a contained manner. After completing the community centre in 1989, I had become quite exhausted by Postmodernism from a stylistic point of view. While still believing in its fundamentals, I went on a "back-to-basics" search and revisited the Modern movement. This resulted in a series of boutique interiors and two houses.

The first house was for the family of Alice Lem, an established interior designer in Singapore. When Lim viewed the house after its completion, he remarked, "Nothing new! We did this thirty years ago!" Indeed, the house, which was painted in white instead of exuberant colours, appeared rather heavy in spite of the lightness and porosity of the interior spaces. FIGS. 7 & 8 Fortunately, another opportunity came along shortly after when the Lems bought another piece of land nearby. This time, I made a much lighter building, Lem's House II (1995–97), using a curtain-wall system on one side of the facade to allow the interior spaces to flow seamlessly to the exterior. FIG. 9 This was complemented by a stunning minimalist interior designed by Lem herself.

Beginning with this latter house, the projects of William Lim Associates began to appear in two different expressions. While Lim still preferred Postmodernism, I adopted a "Neomodern" language, and used it as a starting point for a more individual investigation.[6] These somewhat divergent directions would not have been possible without the open-mindedness and big-heartedness of Lim, for which I am greatly indebted.

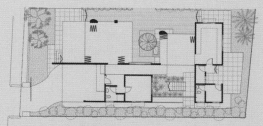

FIG. 7 Lem's House I (1991–93).

FIG. 8 Plan of Lem's House I.

FIG. 9 Lem's House II (1995–97).

5 In the 2000s, the church was extensively renovated by another firm; all the original 1960s finishes as well as our Postmodern elements were completely erased.

6 Architecture critic Leon van Schaik prefers the term "second-order modernism" to "neo-modernism" and used the former to describe my work for Morley Road House. He explained that, while "neo-modernism" suggests an international uniformity, "second-order modernism" signals "a rational approach differing from 'first-order modernism' by the inclusion in the equation of the subjective reality of the designer's and the client's imaginative realm." See his review "Between Abstraction and Cultural Reference: House at Morley Road", *Singapore Architect*, no. 201, 1999, pp. 24–31.

THIS ELEMENT OF DUALITY — REGULAR VERSUS IRREGULAR, ORDERLINESS VERSUS PLAYFULNESS, AND THE WAY THE RICHNESS OF A SPACE IS DESIGNED TO BE CONCEALED AND DISCOVERED — FASCINATES ME TILL THIS DAY.

CHINATOWN INFILL

1981–1982

This was my graduation thesis at the School of Architecture at the National University of Singapore. The conservation proposal was created amidst the rapid redevelopment of the city centre in the 1980s, which ignited a fierce public debate on the importance and viability of conserving the historic buildings within. One such area was Chinatown, an enclave that the former colonial British government had designated from the early nineteenth century for the Chinese immigrants living in Singapore. Over time, this area had extended westward from the northern mouth of the Singapore River to what is currently Maxwell Road.

Chinatown was made up of different areas occupied by the various dialect groups. Its streets were lined with shophouses, a building typology that originated from Southern China's terrace houses, where the ground floors housed businesses and the upper levels were living quarters. My thesis focused on one of the busiest sections of Chinatown known as Kreta Ayer, which means "water cart" in Malay. The name references the bullock and ox carts that used to carry water in an area that has long been a vibrant part of the enclave. Manchu official

Li Chung Chu described it as such in 1887: "There is a place known as Kreta Ayer in 'Greater Town' where restaurants, theatres and brothels are concentrated. It is the most populated area where filth and dirt are hidden. No place in Singapore can compare with it."

My master plan sought to conserve the entirety of Kreta Ayer and create a focal point on a site bounded by three streets: Pagoda Street, which had a concentration of tailors; Temple Street, which had many shops selling ceramic and porcelain wares imported from China; and Trengganu Street, which traverses the two streets and was the centre of activities. Next to the site was a famous opera house, Lai Chun Yuen, that used to face Trengganu Street. The only part of the site not facing a street abuts the back of a gazetted national monument, the Sri Mariamman Temple.

01

01 Aerial view of Kreta Ayer in the late 1970s.

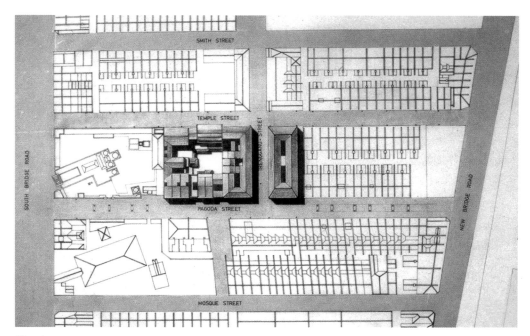

Site plan

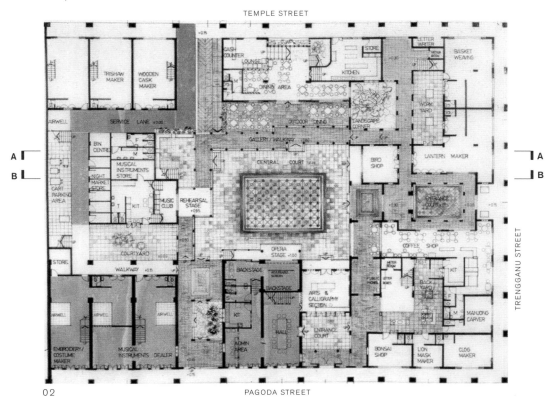

02 First-storey plan showing the various approaches from the surrounding streets to the courtyard.

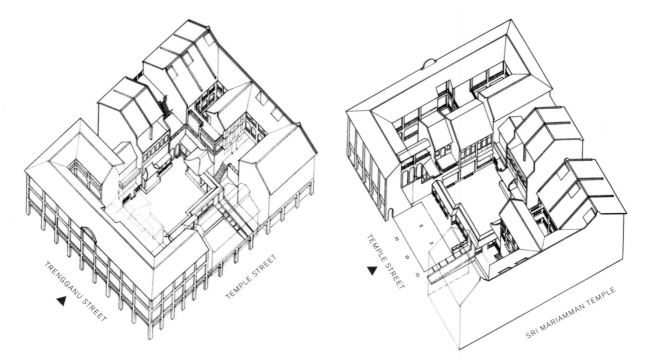

While I proposed keeping the main body of all the shophouses that lined the three streets, the service blocks at the back were to be removed. These faced a narrow, T-shaped back lane, and had been added later to facilitate the removal of night soil. With the removal, the back-lane space would be reconfigured to create a small courtyard inspired by the experience of a classical Chinese garden. This central "garden space" was concealed by the shophouse facades and could be accessed in a variety of manners, depending on where visitors entered from. The approach from Trengganu Street was axial and more formal, while

indirect and meandering routes awaited those coming from Pagoda Street and Temple Street. As visitors journeyed from the streets into the courtyard, they would pass by air wells and small courtyards, as well as shops housing craftspeople making clogs, lion-dance masks, lanterns and other traditional objects.

In the central courtyard, elements like a single-storey roofed corridor and a three-sided open pavilion were introduced. These offered a transition of scale from the surrounding three-storey shophouses, evoking a picturesque quality in the diminutive space.

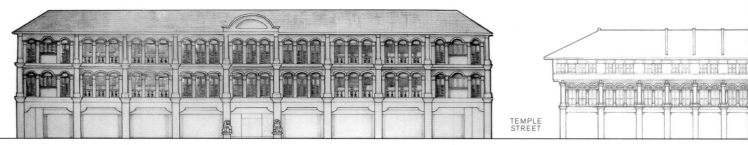

Elevation from Trengganu Street

TEMPLE STREET

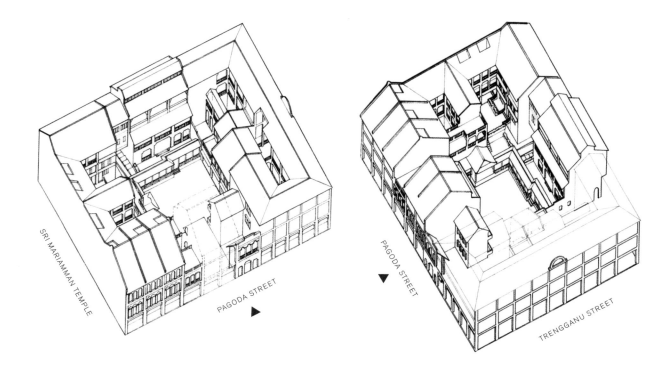

Section AA

Section BB

不夜天

BU YE TIAN

1982

The Singapore River has historically been a hive of activity and the focus of the city-state's development. By the 1980s, however, this area had lost its vigour. The bustling port facilities had been relocated and the adjacent financial district was encroaching into it. As the government considered various proposals to redevelop a section of the riverfront known as Boat Quay, the playwright and poet Dr Goh Poh Seng commissioned us to produce this unsolicited adaptive-reuse scheme.

We proposed to retain a length of about 110 shophouses that had previously been used by the shipping industry for trading and storage. The entire area would then be rejuvenated into a cultural and recreational destination known as Bu Ye Tian (不夜天). Loosely translated from Chinese, this means "a place of ceaseless activity" and was actually the traditional name of the nearby Kreta Ayer but, as this was not remembered by many at the time, Dr Goh was happy to adopt it for this proposal.

While the existing preservation efforts in Singapore were then largely focused on individual buildings, we sought to maintain this 14,500-square-metre (156,000-square-foot) site for traditional activities that remained very much part of Singaporeans' cultural and social life. The two- to three-storey shophouses, mostly constructed in the 1920s and 1930s, would be renovated and converted to restaurants, food stalls, traditional trade and craft shops, workshops, clan associations and a Chinese inn. Existing temporary structures in the back lane would be replaced by an interlinking gallery that offered walkways and a pedestrian arcade with access to the upper floors. There would also be open courtyards, a three-storey tea house and a stage

for traditional Chinese operas known as *wayang*. Boat Quay's riverfront promenade was envisioned as pedestrianized and open for a range of activities, including lion and dragon dances and festivals, as well as open-air markets – all against the backdrop of the river. We also suggested bringing back wooden boats called *tongkangs*, once used for transportation, and converting them into platforms on the river for education and entertainment.

Although Bu Ye Tian was not officially adopted by the government, this ground-up initiative played a major role in accelerating the conservation movement in Singapore. In 1989, the planning authorities announced the conservation of all 110 shophouses. However, instead of carrying out an integrated project as we had proposed, shophouse owners were encouraged to refurbish their own properties, informed by a new set of conservation guidelines. To (re-)introduce a service lane between the two rows of shophouses, all properties were required to have a rear setback, and this led to the removal of the temporary structures that had been haphazardly erected over the years. The government also refurbished the riverfront promenade by pedestrianizing it and providing outdoor dining areas. Today, Boat Quay is a bustling destination for tourists and workers in the nearby financial centre.

01

02

03

04

Drawings by architect. Watercolour renderings by Singapore artist Ong Kim Seng.

01 *Tongkangs* (wooden boats), Singapore River mouth, *c.* 1980s.

02 & 03 Courtyards filled with activities were created by the removal of temporary structures.

04 A covered internal street was introduced between the back-to-back shophouses.

2nd storey

1st storey

Boat Quay elevation

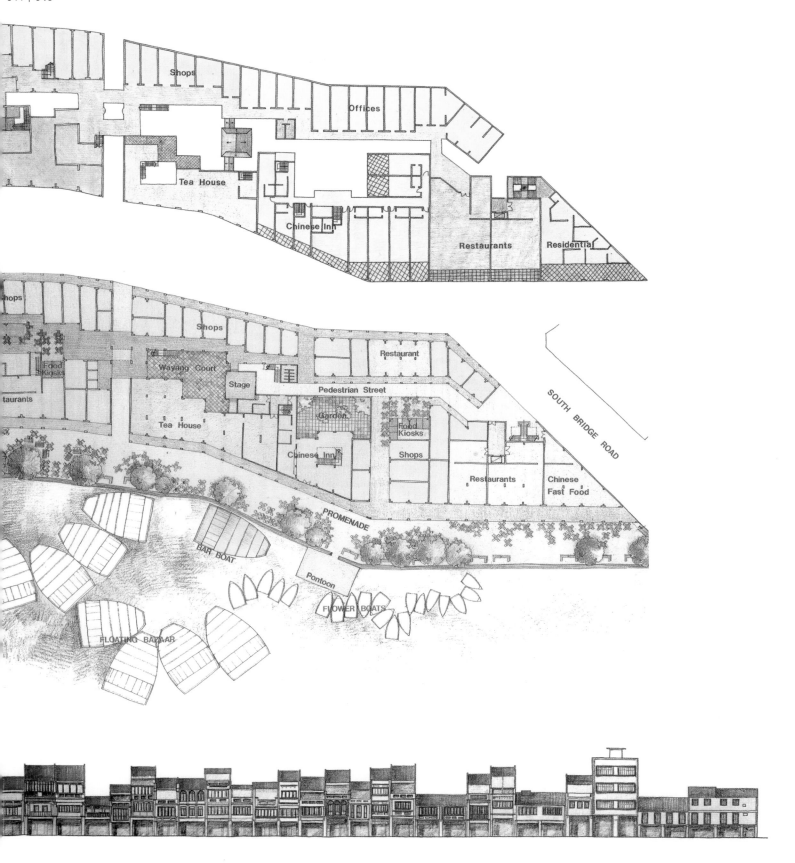

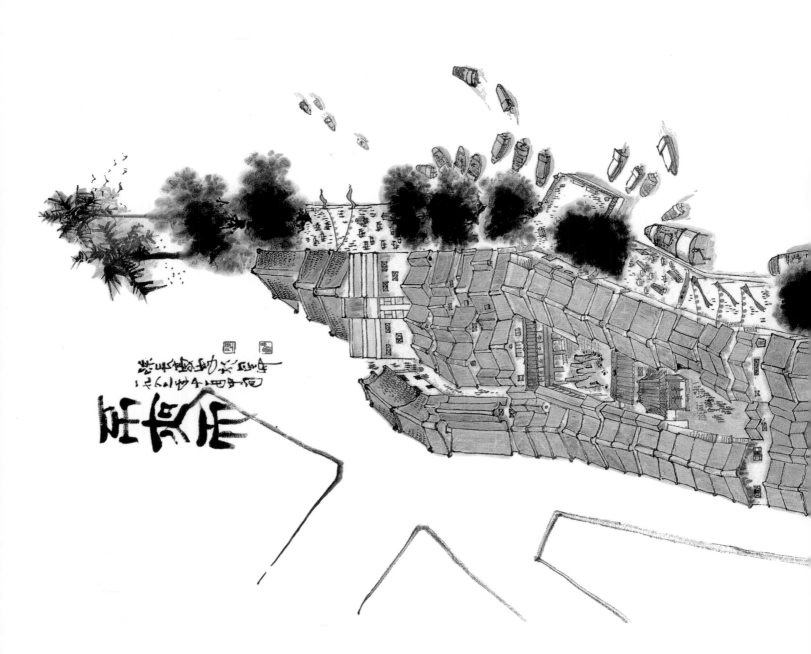

Drawing by architect. Chinese ink rendering by Singapore artist Chan Chang How.

05 Courtyards linked by an internal street were created between the two rows of back-to-back shophouses.

GOH'S HOUSE

1982–1984

This shophouse residence in Emerald Hill was once part of an enclave occupied by rich Peranakan families in Singapore. Its owner, Dr Goh Poh Seng, was a prominent local playwright and poet as well as a Peranakan himself. He had bought this pre-war Straits-Chinese-style townhouse – one of over a hundred in the area – as the family home for himself, his wife Margaret Goh and their four sons. In 1985, a few years after the refurbishment, the government announced that Emerald Hill would be Singapore's first conservation area, as part of its early efforts to preserve historically significant parts of the city.

The building lot had a 5.1-metre (16¾-foot) wide frontage and a depth of 35 metres (115 feet). It was fronted by a covered walkway, traditionally called a five-foot way, which lacked privacy. However, there was a pocket of greenery behind the house, over which two stepped terraces looked out. Our plan places the main living room at the rear, where these terraces are in view, while the kitchen is at the front and next to an intimately scaled entrance lobby –

both face the five-foot way. Taking advantage of newly established conservation guidelines that allowed for a jack roof (an elevated roof segment with a clerestory often found on traditional Southeast-Asian shophouses) and a skylight to be installed on the refurbished tiled roof, we introduced a light well over a pond in the centre of the house. Dr Goh had a collection of carved and gilded timber screens, traditionally used in large Straits-Chinese homes, that he had collected from Penang in Malaysia. These were re-appropriated and integrated to form architectural elements in various parts of the house. They complemented the Southeast-Asian aesthetic of the house, which Dr Goh furnished and decorated himself.

The house was memorable because it was my first built project upon graduation from architecture school. More importantly, the colourful personalities and refined aesthetic sensibilities of the late Gohs left a deep impression on me.

01

02

03

01 Emerald Hill in the 1980s before the townhouses were gazetted for conservation and the street pedestrianized.

02 Facade of the house in the 1980s.

03 A set of gilded Peranakan screens separates the foyer from the dining room.

04

05

04 Central light well.

05 Living room of Goh's House furnished with Southeast-Asian artefacts and crafts.

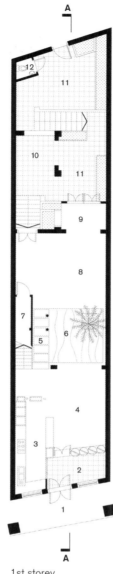

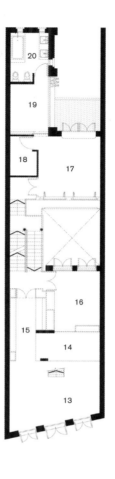

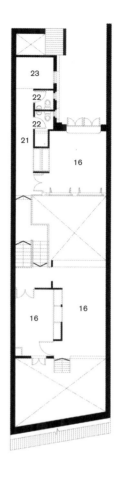

1st storey

2nd storey

3rd storey

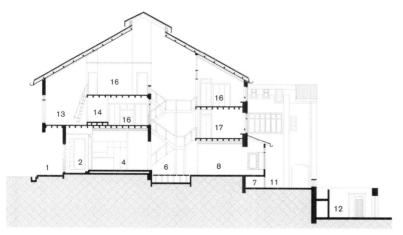

Section AA

1	Five-foot way	13	Family room
2	Foyer	14	Platform
3	Kitchen	15	Library
4	Dining	16	Bedroom
5	Stepping stone	17	Master bedroom
6	Pool	18	Dressing
7	Store	19	Study
8	Living	20	Master bathroom
9	Alcove	21	Corridor
10	Patio	22	Toilet
11	Garden	23	Utility
12	Powder room		

CHURCH OF OUR SAVIOUR

1985 –1987

We converted this former cinema into a house of worship for a church and its rapidly expanding congregation. The brief was for the building to be "nothing like an orthodox church", reflecting this Charismatic church's emphasis on celebration instead of the traditional burden of guilt. It was part of a new movement in Christianity in which the union with God is cause for rejoicing, and this is often expressed in services where singing, spontaneous expressions and rounds of applause are common.

Beginning with a typical 1960s cinema, we added nearly 1,000 square metres (10,500 square feet) of space, mainly in the form of meeting rooms, classrooms and offices. These were largely inserted over the stage area within the building, as the existing cinema was already built close to its setback lines on three sides. On the fourth side, facing an open car park that had been reserved for future expansion, spaces were added as a series of attachments onto the facade. On one end, the pastor's office was housed within a wavy rust-red wall unit with a flat roof, and this was mounted on purple-inverted cone columns. Across the length of the facade was a rectangular office space topped with a pitched roof. These geometrically diverse forms sticking out from the existing box were partly inspired by the look of the then wildly popular Italian Memphis style. They also complemented the vibrant spirit of the church's mode of worship. The celebratory expression also extended to all the building's exuberant finishes. Part of these came from the cinema's original design, which included mosaic tiles used in various coloured patterns as well as a blue-and-silver chequered ceiling. Instead of demolishing these features, which were commonly viewed as outdated and "cheap" at the time, we retained them out of practical budget constraints and also to elevate such materials.

While the effusive exterior may not come across as church-like, there was no ambiguity inside the building. The acoustics of the voluminous hall were rebalanced to resonate sound instead of absorbing it so as to amplify the praises and glorifications during service. This was complemented by painting the hall in various shades of white to give a sense of being uplifted – in spite of there being no windows at all. Although the hall had no cross, there was a collection of signs that visually expressed that it was a church. We appropriated an existing series of aluminium spheres complete with encircling orbits that had previously symbolized the namesake of the theatre, Venus. These motifs on one side of the wall were accompanied by an ornamental pillar shaped like a bolt of lightning and cloud-like cascading walls with sawtooth edges. Together, these "celestial" elements generated a multidirectional vista that brought out the theme of creation.

01

02

03

01 View of original cinema building, completed in 1965.

02 & 03 View of the new additions expressed in
exuberant forms and colours.

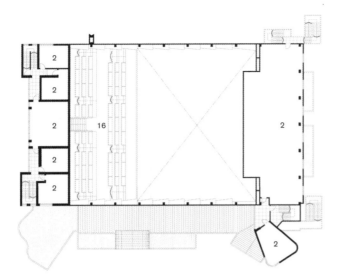

3rd storey

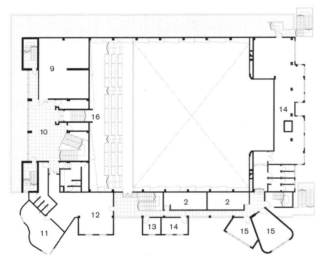

2nd storey

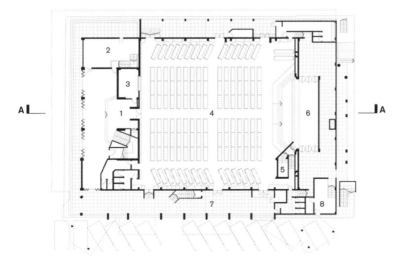

A|——   ——|A

1st storey

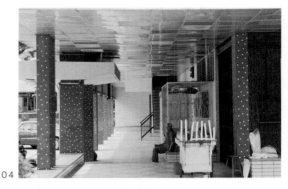

04

05

1	Foyer	10	Upper lobby
2	Classroom	11	Pastor's office
3	Sound control room	12	Administration office
4	Main sanctuary	13	Printing room
5	Baptismal pool	14	Pastoral room
6	Stage	15	Meeting room
7	Veranda	16	Upper sanctuary
8	Caretaker's room		(access at 2nd storey)
9	Home cell	17	Basement
	leaders' room		

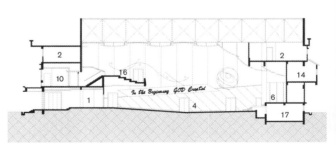

Section AA

06

07

04 View of the original veranda with the 1960s palette of finishes.

05 The original rear facade.

06 View of renovated veranda, where new finishes interact with the existing ones.

07 Protruding additions on the rear facade.

TAMPINES NORTH COMMUNITY CENTRE AND EXTENSION

1986–1989
1990–1992

Contained within the strict order of this building's perimeter is a colourful collage of blocks that come in assorted shapes and sizes. These two different elements contrast yet complement each other to form this community facility designed for residents of Tampines New Town.

Located on a roughly rectangular site, the centre is bound by a three-storey-high frame of regularly spaced twin columns. This echoes the ordered facades of the surrounding public-housing apartment blocks. However, to distinguish our centre from their plaster-and-paint facades, we used glass-block infill as it has no colour and is a self-finished material.

This "circulation frame" also contains a corridor linking the centre's four main blocks and two smaller ones, each of which houses specific activities ranging from sports amenities to recreation rooms.

The largest block is a multi-purpose hall that takes up a third of the centre and sits on one end of the frame. The remaining activity blocks each come in different shapes and sizes, and are arranged to encourage the circulation of air and to offer diagonal secondary routes across the centre. Fittingly, the main entrance building adopts an obtrusive and irregular form that bursts through the tight frame to welcome residents.

A few years after the building was completed, we were invited to make extensions on the roof spaces to cater to its growing popularity. A cable-tensioned steel roof was designed to cover the entrance building for public celebrations and activities. Comprising three identical strips of curved steel sheet arranged in staggered formation, this wave-like structure caps the uninhibited forms found throughout the centre.

01

02

01 Aerial view of the community centre situated within a public-housing estate.

02 Key architectural elements of the community centre, with a public-housing block behind.

03

04

05

03 The centre is bound by a three-storey-high frame of regularly spaced twin columns.

04 The irregular form of the entrance block contrasts with the ordered circulation structure.

05 The corridor that encircles the building is set behind the twin-columned frame.

06

07

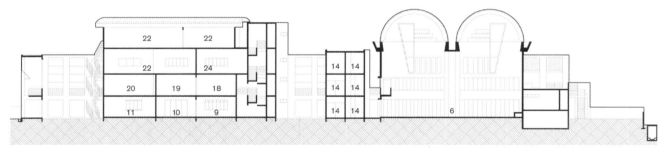

Section AA

08

06 Courtyard spaces between free-standing buildings.

07 View of courtyard space bounded by the circulation frame.

08 The column-free space under a new roof suspended
by tension cables.

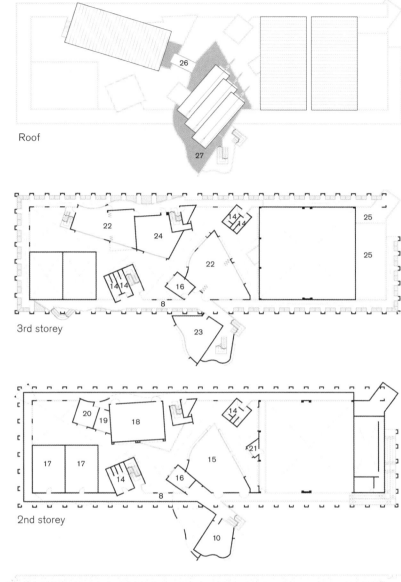

Roof

3rd storey

2nd storey

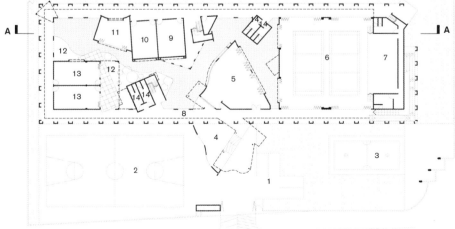

1st storey

1   Car park
2   Basketball court
3   Sepak takraw court
4   Sitting area
5   Office
6   Multi-purpose hall
7   Stage
8   Circulation frame
9   Health and fitness
10 Homecraft
11 Lounge
12 Sandpit
13 Kindergarten
14 Toilet
15 Reading room
16 Committee room
17 Squash courts
18 Dance studio
19 Dark room
20 Music room
21 AV room
22 Multi-purpose room
23 Conference room
24 Arts and craft room
25 Roof
26 Link bridge
27 Covered roof terrace

LEM'S HOUSE II

1995 – 1997

The design of this house makes the best out of its site. Sitting at the end of a cul-de-sac, it looks north and east over a tidal drainage canal and is cooled by daily breezes from the coast. Besides the canal, there are no other views of significance in any direction.

Our three-storey house takes full advantage of this singular view with a glazed curtain wall that is framed in aluminium. This is carried out on its north-east-facing elevation, as well as a considerable amount of its south-east and north-west portions, the latter of which overlooks a playground. While this allows pedestrians and cyclists using the promenade along the canal – just 10 metres (33 feet) away from the house – to look directly inside, the owner was prepared to accept such transparency in exchange for an unobstructed view of the canal. In sharp contrast to this openness, the west and south-west facades of the house are solid walls that protect it from the afternoon and evening sun. They also turn the back of the house towards its immediate neighbours and the rest of the estate.

A simple orthogonal plan was adopted and the house had to be split along the "fracture line" to fit its tapering site. One part of the plan slides along this fracture to accommodate the wider portion, and this is emphasized in the formal massing of the house. On the north side, vertical wall planes expressed as projections suggest multiple fracture lines. Entering the house from the car porch, one encounters a shallow pond that extends from the side of the entrance lobby into the garden in front of the study and alongside the dining room. This "moat" brings the surroundings into the interior conceptually. With its flat roofs, planar form and aluminium-framed windows, this home was very different from my previous Postmodernist architecture as found in the Church of Our Saviour (1985–87) or Tampines North Community Centre (1986–89). It represented a turning point in my practice – towards a Neomodernist architectural language.

01

02

03

01 The glazed facade that overlooks a waterway.

02 View of the house from the cul-de-sac.

03 Deep overhanging eaves and sunshades shield the glazed facade from the morning sun.

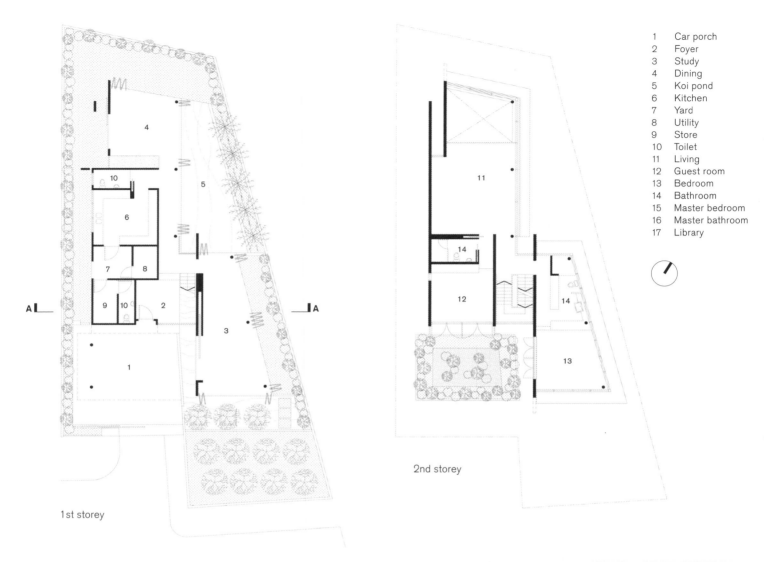

1st storey

2nd storey

1 Car porch
2 Foyer
3 Study
4 Dining
5 Koi pond
6 Kitchen
7 Yard
8 Utility
9 Store
10 Toilet
11 Living
12 Guest room
13 Bedroom
14 Bathroom
15 Master bedroom
16 Master bathroom
17 Library

04 Reflecting pond along the length of the house.
05 Flow of spaces from indoor to outdoor and beyond.
06 View of the waterway from second-storey living room.
07 A west-facing solid facade.

04

05

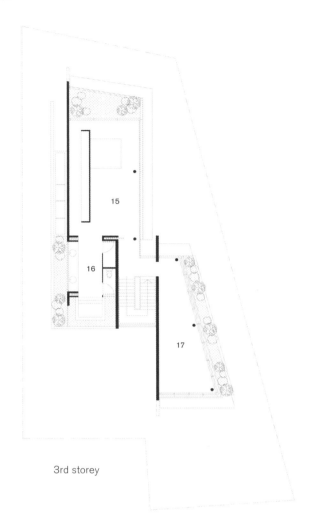

3rd storey

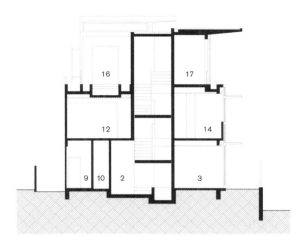

Section AA

06

07

02

RESPOND

CONTEXTUALISM
IN A CONSTRICTING
ENVIRONMENT

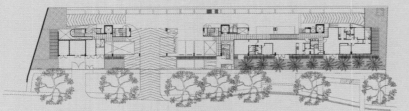

FIG. 1 The long, narrow footprint of The Paterson Edge (1996–99).

FIG. 2 The Arris (1997–2003) on its slim triangular plot.

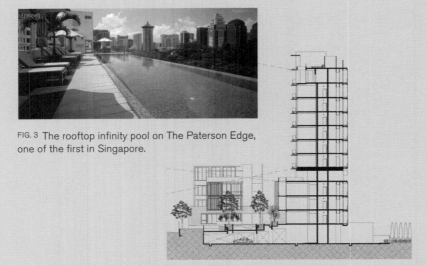

FIG. 3 The rooftop infinity pool on The Paterson Edge, one of the first in Singapore.

FIG. 4 Differentiation of the lower and upper massings of Three Three Robin (2000–6).

FIG. 5 The first three levels of The Nassim (2006–15) are expressed as landscape decks.

Working in Singapore requires us to constantly grapple with limitations. Since the 1960s, the city-state's population has grown from just under 2 million to reach 5.79 million in 2018. With a land area of just 719 square kilometres (278 square miles), Singapore's population density stands at 7,796 per square kilometre (20,827 per square mile), making it the second densest sovereign state in the world. This has conditioned Singaporeans to treat land as a scarce resource, and its city planners prescribe densities, uses and building heights for every available piece of land. Given Singapore's geographic location, there is also the underlying need to respond to the tropical climate, which can make living uncomfortable. Our approach to these constraints has always been to respond contextually, and regard them as impetus for our designs.

Growing with a Denser City

In the mid-1990s, we applied the Neomodernist language of Lem's House II (1995–97) to a series of larger-scale housing projects. These often sat on tight, challenging sites, and within densely built-up environments. The Paterson Edge (1996–99) FIG. 1 and The Arris (1997–2003) FIG. 2 were two such early commissions, catering to the niche market created by a growing demographic of singles and couples opting to live in the heart of the city. Both projects saw us seek a reduction in the requisite boundary setback from the planning authority so as to realize the full quantum of floor space allowed. The resulting buildings contain small apartments compacted into tight building envelopes, and the consequent lack of ground space led to the inclusion of rooftop features such as pools with panoramic views. FIG. 3 These were among the earliest examples of such lifestyle features in the city, which have since become commonplace in similar developments.

Two later projects demonstrate how we utilize massing when designing in dense neighbourhoods. In Three Three Robin (2000–6), we split the massing of the building into two distinct parts to offer good views in a congested neighbourhood. While the lower section avoided the view of an adjacent four-storey apartment block, instead facing inwards to an intimate communal space, the upper portion was positioned to offer unobstructed views. FIG. 4 In The Nassim (2006–15), the scale of the five-storey apartment blocks was reduced so that the lower three floors read as tiered landscape decks; above these sit the upper two floors, which were expressed as "houses". FIG 5 This allowed us to meet the client's demand for a dense development inspired by the "black and white bungalows" popular among Europeans in Singapore during the early twentieth century.

Some fifteen years after this adoption of a Neomodernist language, the expression had gained popularity and become the mainstream architectural style in Singapore. We began expanding beyond the approach of using strict orthogonal geometries and compositional planes and lines. The change was not about mere surface treatment, but exploring new design expressions grounded on a sound basis. This was particularly so when addressing Singapore's rapidly increasing density. From the mid-1990s, the city-state added a million people to its population every decade – achieved largely through immigration – a figure that it had previously taken some three decades to reach. In response to this, we began employing "elevated groundscapes" in our work. This strategy of creating more "ground space" within the same footprint of a development allowed us to create valuable and desirable spaces, as well as redefine the traditional approaches to spatial relationships. Coupled with the search for a new expression, we began developing an architectural language integral to this concept.

The first experimentation took place in the Extension of Paya Lebar Methodist Girls' Secondary School (2004–7), where an elevated "new ground" was created by introducing a large floor plate at the third level of the school. This covered an entire portion of the site, upon which a new theatre and games courts were built. FIG. 6 With this approach, we could create space for these programmes, which could not have been fitted on the real ground. Following the irregular shape of the site, this "new ground" took on an organic geometry, independent of the rectilinear configuration of the teaching blocks that sat below and above it. Since then, we've also brought this approach to our residential projects. For The Oliv (2007–13), small communal landscaped spaces were planned in front of every duplex apartment in this twelve-storey block. This effectively extends their "grounds", bringing residents one step closer to the ideal of living in "bungalows in the sky". FIG. 7 In contrast with the rectilinear apartment block, The Oliv's landscaped decks were treated as undulating terrains accentuated with textured and natural materials. FIG. 8 Similarly, 11 Kim Tian Road (2013–18) has a 200-metre-long (656-foot-long) elevated communal deck that was created by linking up the roofs of four low-rise residential blocks. This landscaped deck, which was dotted with amenities, was expressed as an organic element that stood in contrast with the development's regular residential towers. FIG. 9

FIG. 6 The elevated floor plate at Paya Lebar Methodist Girls' Secondary School (2004–7).

FIG. 7 In The Oliv (2007–13), living spaces are extended by the introduction of sky terraces.

FIG. 8 The elevated, undulating "terrain" of The Oliv's sky terraces.

FIG. 9 The 200m- (656ft-) long elevated communal deck, 11 Kim Tian Road (2013–18).

FIG. 10 The sleek glass facade of The Paterson Edge ...

FIG. 11 ... and of The Arris.

The underlying tone exemplified in these projects is our approach towards design renewal: retaining fundamentals that are relevant, while adding on new layers of expression that arise out of changing conditions.

Innovation in Spite of Regulations

Even though the practice is selective in the number of jobs we undertake, the bulk of our work is housing projects, as these are the dominant form of development in Singapore's private sector. This means we have to constantly search for new design impetus to sustain the creative drive for this building typology. Beyond site conditions, Singapore's mundane yet extensive building regulations provide an unlikely source of creative possibilities. They are overseen by the city's Urban Redevelopment Authority (URA), which sees urban planning as very much an integral part of economic development in land-scarce Singapore. Over the decades, the agency has continuously reviewed its regulations to ensure good living conditions, even with high densities.

One major change in the planning parameters occurred in the late 1980s, when the URA revised its long-standing practice of determining the quantum of a site using density and the number of people that can be accommodated. Instead, there was now a prescribed plot ratio over a piece of land to compute the allowable gross floor area (GFA). This was intended to give flexibility in the provision of different sizes of dwelling units, and to better control the bulk of the massing. However, the unintended consequence was that, given an absolute allowable GFA, property developers quickly latched onto the strategy of minimizing the provision of common areas (read: unsaleable) in order to maximize saleable areas, and thus their profits. As a result, no architect in Singapore can remain in practice today without mastering the art of "efficient" design.

Up until the 1980s, the regulatory framework also did not encourage any integration between nature and buildings. Singapore's fame as a "Garden City" was still confined to an elaborate tree-planting programme that seemed only to focus on lining the roads and filling the parks with trees. But, with the government's increasing ambition in the mid-1990s to remodel the city as one with a living environment conducive to attracting global talent, we witnessed a series of changes in the building guidelines. Over the span of just a decade, policies that impeded the creation of even basic tropical living spaces have evolved to encourage the proliferation of communal garden spaces in high-rise buildings.

Our housing projects have captured this evolution. The sleek glass skins that formed the facades of The Paterson Edge FIG. 10 and The Arris FIG. 11 were a reaction to the guidelines that disincentivized the provision of balconies, as their presence meant fewer enclosed saleable spaces, which no developer would accept. But, when the planning authorities introduced an additional ten per cent of bonus GFA as an incentive for the provision of balconies, they became a feature on the facade of later developments such as Three Three Robin. FIG. 12 In the mid-2000s, planners gave further GFA exemption incentives to encourage the introduction of elevated communal green spaces in the form of sky terraces. The Oliv pushed that regulation to its limit with the creation of a facade of stacked gardens. FIG. 13

Responding to frequent regulatory changes, designing with "tricks" to enhance saleable areas, while also being mindful of opportunities to create architectural delights, has become a necessary skill among Singapore architects. As architecture critic Leon van Schaik observed in an internal review of one of our projects in 2004:

> That this [innovation] is in the apartment buildings conducted in a context that is remorselessly driven by the mathematics of GFA and the regulatory framework that makes architects in Singapore mandarins in the arts of interpreting rules and what they allow – whatever the intentions of their original framers – makes this innovation all the more impressive.

FIG. 12 Balconies with sliding screens at Three Three Robin.

FIG. 13 The facade of The Oliv is a manifestation of the sky-terrace guideline.

FIG. 14 Void decks used as social spaces in early public-housing developments.

FIG. 15 A Malay wedding celebration in a public-housing void deck.

FIG. 16 The entrances of the UOB Plaza (1992) in the city centre feature a covered and open public space.

FIG. 17 Busy covered parade square at the Paya Lebar school extension project.

FIG. 18 The covered open-study area at the Education Resource Centre (2008–11).

Creating Spaces for a Tropical City

In his 1995 essay "Singapore Songlines", architect Rem Koolhaas observed: "The irony of Singapore's climate is that its tropical heat and humidity are at the same time the perfect alibi for a full-scale retreat into interior, generalized, non-specific, air-conditioned comfort – and the sole surviving element of authenticity, the only thing that makes Singapore tropical, still." While this criticism was, to a certain extent, valid at the time, the situation has since changed significantly. It is a reality that heat and humidity can be very uncomfortable in the Tropics when not mediated, and air-conditioned environments are as necessary as heated environments are for temperate climates. However, it is important to introduce a sequence of transition zones from the exterior to the interior and to celebrate them. When designed well, such covered and open-sided in-between spaces are the most comfortable for the Tropics. These range from verandas in houses to the void decks in many early public-housing flats. FIGS. 14 & 15 Increasingly, they can also be found in the covered and open public spaces in Singapore's city centre as well as its outskirts. One of the earliest examples is the UOB Plaza at the mouth of the Singapore River, completed in 1992. FIG. 16

Over the years, we have conceptualized and realized such in-between spaces in our projects too. At the Extension of Paya Lebar Methodist Girls' Secondary School, the "elevated ground" that we introduced turned the traditionally open-to-sky assembly ground into a covered open space. Shielded from the tropical sun, the girls can now comfortably utilize the space for all kinds of activities throughout the day. FIG. 17 When designing the National University of Singapore's Education Resource Centre (2008–11), we proposed to reduce the provision of air-conditioned study areas by thirty per cent, and replaced them with covered open spaces distributed over various parts of the centre. These are protected by deep overhangs to keep the sun and the rain out, and are well integrated with the greenery all round. The most popular of these transition zones is a double-volume study area that faces the Town Green, an open-recreational area at the heart of the campus.

Located along a breezeway, this study area is usually filled with students appropriately dressed in shorts and T-shirts. In fact, it has proven to be as popular as the air-conditioned Starbucks café located next to it, if not more so. FIG. 18

Our competition entry for Singapore's School of the Arts in 2005 expressed the creation of in-between spaces as part of an urban scale. We proposed a four-storey teaching facility that sat on a large floor plate equivalent to the entire site, but lifted 20 metres (66 feet) above ground. Underneath was a big volume expressed like an urban cavern, strategically filled with public and commercial programmes. Designed for public access, this was meant to draw in the flow of pedestrian movement, as the school sat at the confluence of the Orchard Road shopping belt, the arts and cultural district of Bras Basah and Singapore's historical Civic District. It would in fact act like a covered park for the city. FIG. 19 With this proposal, we envisaged a district where existing buildings in the surrounding area could collectively form an urban system. The naturally ventilated atrium at the LASALLE College of the Arts, the void deck at the National Library and the urban corridor of the National Museum of Singapore would all come together to impart an identity to the district and allow for unique experiences. FIG. 20

We have in many architectural forums advocated that the image of Singapore should not be signposted by iconic buildings. Instead, it should be formed by the collective presence of these covered open public spaces.[1] Compared to erecting buildings as icons, creating public spaces to form an archetypal urban identity can be equally powerful, memorable and, in a tropical city, definitely more enjoyable.

FIG. 19 A covered urban park was proposed for the School of the Arts competition entry (2005).

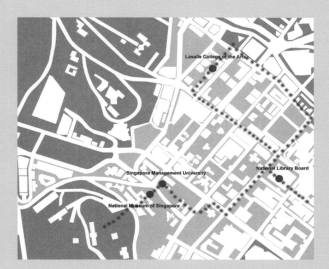

FIG. 20 The image of the city formed by a series of covered and open public spaces.

[1] The idea of "spaces as icons" is a reaction against the current trend of cities using eye-catching "iconic" structures to stand out in an increasingly competitive global network. It builds upon some of the earlier urban-design strategies speculated by proponents of "tropical design". These include Singaporean architect Tay Kheng Soon's *Mega-Cities in the Tropics: Towards an Architectural Agenda for the Future* (Singapore: Institute of Southeast Asian Studies, 1989) and Malaysian architect Ken Yeang's *The Tropical Verandah City: Some Urban Design Ideas for Kuala Lumpur* (Petaling Jaya: Longman, 1987).

WORKING IN SINGAPORE
REQUIRES US TO
CONSTANTLY GRAPPLE
WITH LIMITATIONS …
OUR APPROACH TO
THESE CONSTRAINTS
HAS ALWAYS BEEN TO
RESPOND CONTEXTUALLY,
AND REGARD THEM
AS IMPETUS FOR
OUR DESIGNS.

THE PATERSON EDGE

1996–1999

After years of refurbishing shophouses, we were presented with this opportunity that eventually helped us break into the residential-development market. Located on the edge of Singapore's major shopping street, Orchard Road, this project was on an extremely narrow rectangular configuration that was only 100 metres (328 feet) long and 8 metres (26 feet) wide. We even had to negotiate with the planning authorities to reduce the stipulated setback so as to create small yet liveable apartments for singles and couples.

The highly restrictive site led us to adopt a full-scale curtain wall, which is stretched taut along its eastern boundary. This flatness expressed our inability to accommodate any kind of projections on the facade – not even balconies, a feature that the planning authorities only encouraged years later with a series of incentives. The glass facade also helped the units look bigger by offering residents an expansive view of the city. In exchange, their lifestyles were on display to drivers along the six-lane Paterson Road, as well as to pedestrians on a narrow walkway. Screened only by sun fins, blinds and a row of mature rain trees alongside the building, this transparent design caused quite a stir when it was first revealed!

In contrast, the western side of this twelve-storey building offers an opaque facade to the low-rise residential area it overlooks. This solid surface shields the development from the setting sun and also conceals its service ducts. Left with no space on the ground for amenities, we placed an edgeless lap pool on the rooftop, which offers stunning views of the city. This was the first such snazzy roof in Singapore, particularly at a time when such a space was more commonly used for services.

In form, material and language, The Paterson Edge's clean lines of steel and glass are an augmentation of Lem's House II (1995–97). All sixty apartments were sold within days of its launch, and this signalled to developers that we could deliver on residential developments, offering excellent contemporary designs in spite of very difficult sites.

01

01 Transparent living.

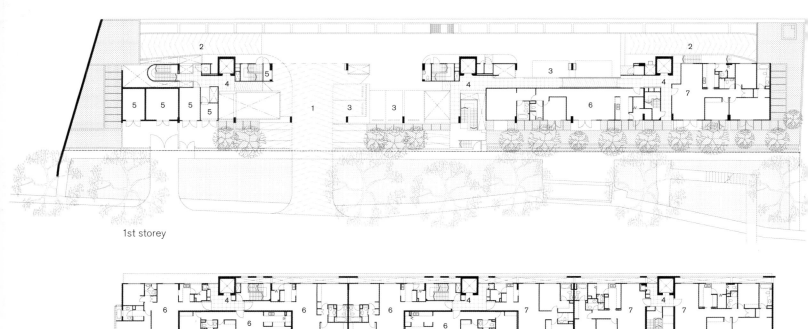

1st storey

Typical storey

Roof

1	Driveway	6	2-bedroom unit
2	Ramp to and from basement car park	7	3-bedroom unit
3	Car park	8	Roof terrace
4	Lift lobby	9	Swimming pool
5	M&E rooms	10	Swimming pool deck
		11	Putting green

02 Rear facade with vertical and horizontal concrete sunshades.

03 A glazed facade with horizontal sunshades faces the main road.

02

03

04

04 The play of light on the glazed facade filtered through the sunshades.

05 Horizontal sunshades.

06 The living space as part of the larger city.

05

06

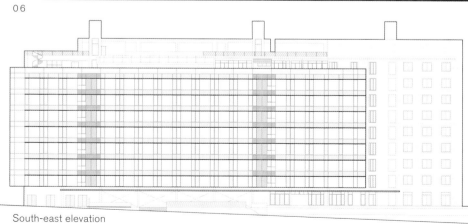

South-east elevation

07 OVERLEAF The rooftop edgeless pool looks out to the city skyline.

THE LOFT

1996–2002

A series of careful negotiations with existing elements on the site led to this inward-looking residence. This cluster of seventy-seven apartments retains much of its natural surroundings, offering a peaceful sanctuary on the edge of Singapore's main shopping street, Orchard Road.

We overcame the tight, triangular-shaped site and a four-storey height restriction by using perimeter planning to achieve a fairly dense plot ratio of 1:1.4. But, unlike this method's conventional continuous extrusion, we fragmented the plan to conserve nine mature trees dotted along the site's boundaries. The resulting ring of five blocks is linked by a series of glass-walled bridges that deftly manoeuvre around the trees while framing views of them. To create a focal point in the plan, one of the blocks was also skewed and differentiated with a full-facade trellis planted with climbers.

Our design cuts the site, which slopes almost 9 metres (30 feet) across, into an upper and lower deck. This called for the use of a wall along the split, which is transformed into this development's signature element. Stretching 50 metres (164 feet) wide and 5 metres (16 feet) high, the wall serves as a navigational spine and also visually anchors the base of the block furthest away from Nassim Hill Road.

As the wall shields the upper level of the development's two-storey car park, planning regulations then required it to be softened by tiered planters. However, we convinced the authorities to allow an exposed granite wall. This is intermittently landscaped with slots of Kyoto Dwarf Grass to reduce the wall's scale and emphasize its horizontality. Such a monolithic feature stands out from the apartments, which are white-washed and accentuated by steel trellises and glazed curtain walls. This transparent inner skin contrasts with the solid exterior. Surrounding the development are walls with strategic cuts-outs, protecting the privacy of residents yet also offering teasing glances into the oasis within.

02

01 A conserved tree marks the entrance to the development.

02 The perimeter massing is split to allow for the conservation of a mature tree.

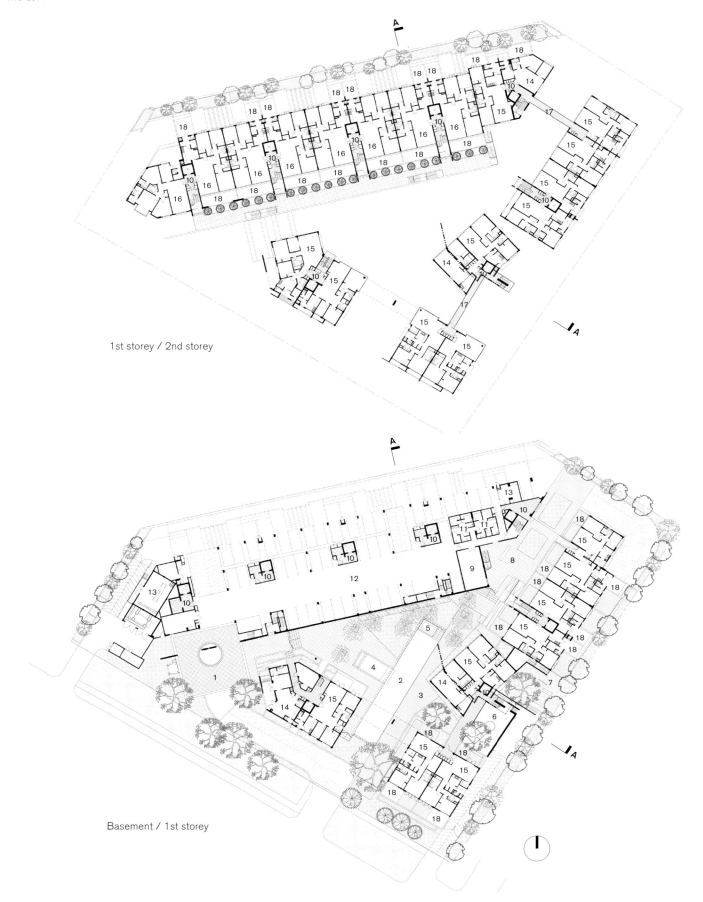

1st storey / 2nd storey

Basement / 1st storey

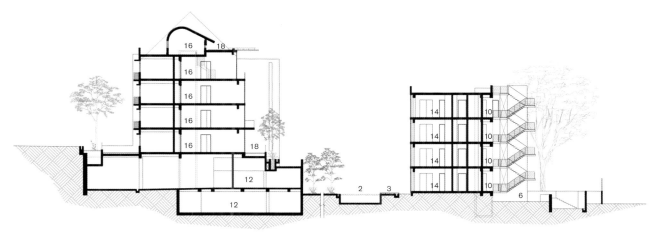

Section A A

1	Entrance court	10	Lift lobby
2	Swimming pool	11	Steam, sauna and changing rooms
3	Swimming pool deck	12	Basement car park
4	Children's pool	13	M&E rooms
5	Jacuzzi pool	14	1-bedroom unit
6	Children's play area	15	2-bedroom unit
7	Fitness corner	16	3-bedroom unit
8	BBQ area	17	Link bridge
9	Gym	18	Private terrace

03

04

03 Building facade viewed from the entrance court.

04 Articulated stairways on the main building's facade.

06

07

05 The two-tiered courtyard features a stone-clad wall along the split.

06 The upper deck of the courtyard.

07 Facade of the main building, which sits on the upper deck.

08 The perimeter block is fragmented on plan to conserve
mature trees and is linked by glazed bridges. One of the blocks
is positioned askew to accommodate a tree behind it.

09

09 The facade of the skewed block is differentiated with trellis to act as a focal point in the courtyard.

10

11

10 & 12 Glass bridges deftly manoeuvre around the trees while also framing views of them.

11 Details of the trellis.

12

13 The development's roofscape.

THE ARRIS

1997 – 2003

The success of The Paterson Edge (1996–99) led its client to commission a similar residential development along Yan Kit Road. Faced with yet another tight site, we borrowed ideas from the previous project to design this ten-storey apartment block.

A taut glass curtain wall is again deployed as a boundary along the eastern end of the site. This reflects the tall mature roadside trees beside the road, and at the same time presents an impenetrable surface. In contrast, the western side of the development is a solid volume that shields it from the sun. This stark feature was mandatory, allowing the building's setback to be reduced by a metre (3 feet) so as to maximize the footprint. Midway through the design process, we took advantage of updates in planning regulations to provide some relief in the form of a series of small windows.

Behind its glazed facade, the building rises up in an amorphous form to satisfy the brief for small apartments within this triangular site. While the broader 40-metre (130-foot) northern end allowed for standard-size floor plates, we had to squeeze small studio apartments into the narrower half, which

tapers 38 degrees into a sharp edge. The result is a development split into two blocks with a shift between them. Between the split is a discreet pedestrian entryway that leads through the building to its rear. By detaching the mass of the building footprint at the rear and reconnecting the different elements with bridges and platforms, we also opened up breathing voids around and on the lower levels of the confined site.

The two apartment blocks rise up seven floors together before they are staggered to accommodate an additional three-storey element perched above. This stepped profile not only reduces the scale of the building when seen from the street, but also allows for various additional features. On the broader block, we created a series of roof terraces – which were exempted from the Gross Floor Area calculation – for the apartments on the eighth storey, while the narrower block has a cantilevered lap pool that offers views of the city centre.

01

01 A series of solid volumes faces the western sun. Minimal openings on the facade helped to reduce the setback by a metre (3 ft) to gain space for the development.

02 The development sits on a tight triangular site.

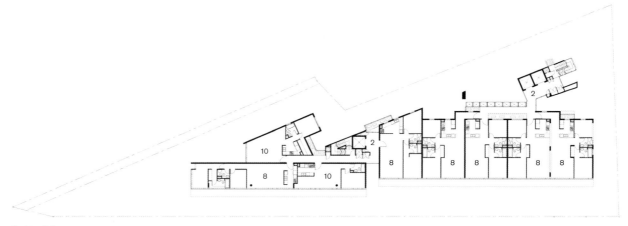

3rd to 6th storey

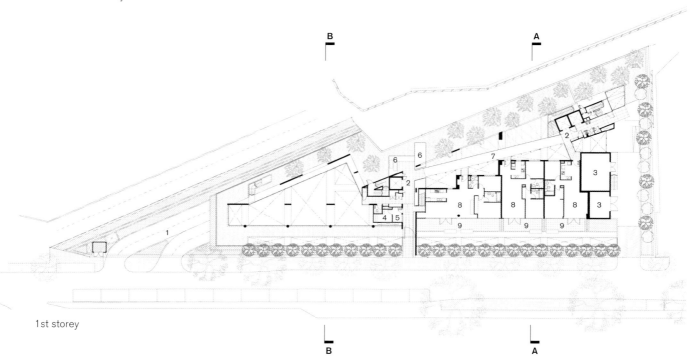

1st storey

1	Driveway	6	Water feature
2	Lift lobby	7	Link bridge
3	M&E rooms	8	2-bedroom unit
4	Guardhouse	9	Private terrace
5	Management office	10	1-bedroom unit

03 A taut glass curtain wall defines the boundary facing the street.

03

04

05

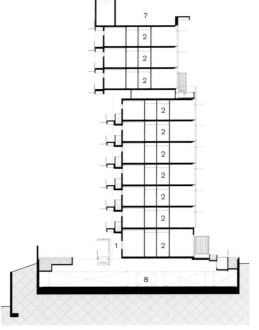

Section AA

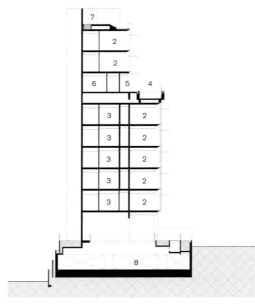

Section BB

1	Link bridge
2	2-bedroom unit
3	1-bedroom unit
4	Swimming pool
5	Swimming pool deck
6	Gym
7	Terrace
8	Basement car park

04 & 05 Views from basement: voids created on the ground-floor slab reduce unused Gross Floor Area, and bring light into the basement car park.

06 Voids created on the ground floor resulted in an isolated slab, expressed as a bridge connecting two lift lobbies.

06

07 The stepped profile, a response to building-height and setback controls, allows for the introduction of amenities in the development.

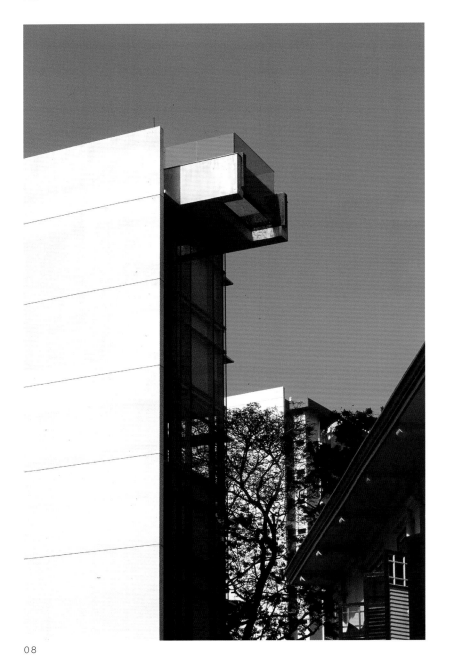

08

09

08 Cantilevered pool.

09 Shaded walkway leading to the swimming pool and gym.

11

10 Curtain-wall facade with sun-shading fins.
11 Private terraces overlooking the city.

THREE THREE ROBIN

2000–2006

The need to offer good views amidst a densely built-up neighbourhood resulted in the massing concept of this residence. Three low-rise buildings are set off against a main apartment block – a combination of two different scales and forms in a single development.

The central organizing element is a medium-rise slab block, but significant changes in shape, scale and form were carried out on and around its first three levels. This is where a pool and lush landscape serve not just as a communal area but also provide intimate views for a series of three small "houses" encircling the main block. In a visually surprising change of scale, the block then rises above this landscape deck to take in unobstructed views of the surroundings.

As the preferred north–south orientation had views obstructed by nearby buildings, the apartment block was placed in an east–west position instead. This is not a desirable solar orientation for the Tropics, but we installed extensive timber-louvred sliding panels on the building's western facade to deal with the sun and also impart a warmth and textural richness. In contrast, its eastern exterior is exposed, with its clean and linear facade made up of horizontal fins, thin planters and glass sliding doors that offer a large degree of transparency.

Such a duality in experience also awaits visitors to the development. Entering through a long driveway – lined with tall slender conical trees to hint at its exclusivity – they arrive at an understated entrance court. As they head up the stairs to the communal area, a lush, leafy oasis reveals itself, offering a respite from this congested neighbourhood of high-rise developments.

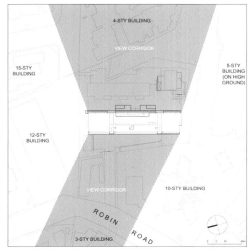

02

01 OPPOSITE A sun-shaded facade greets the approach to the development. All photographs were taken in 2019.

02 The apartment block is placed in an east–west orientation to take advantage of the view corridors on either side.

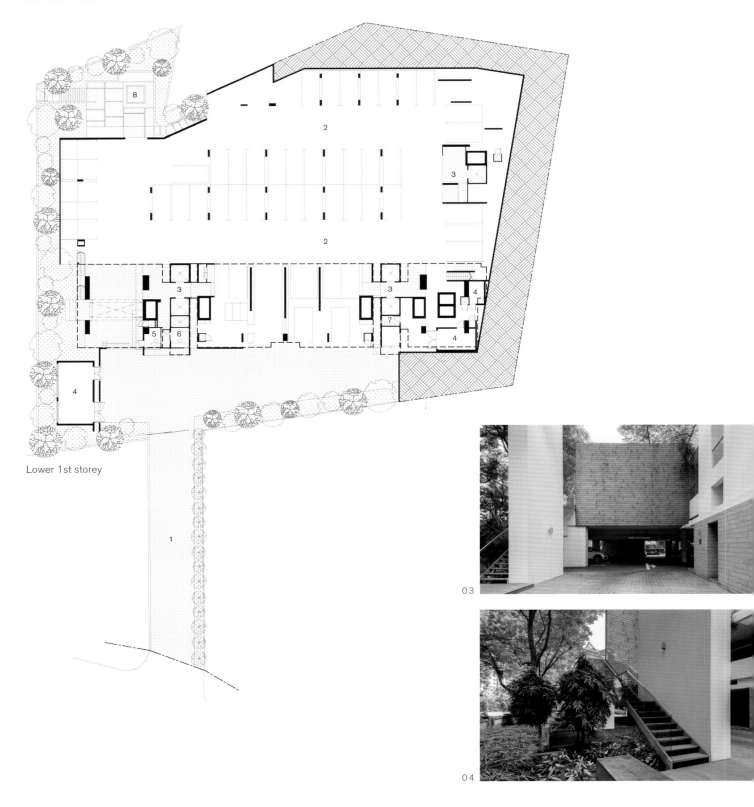

Lower 1st storey

03 Entry to lower first-storey car park.

04 Stairway leading to first-storey communal area.

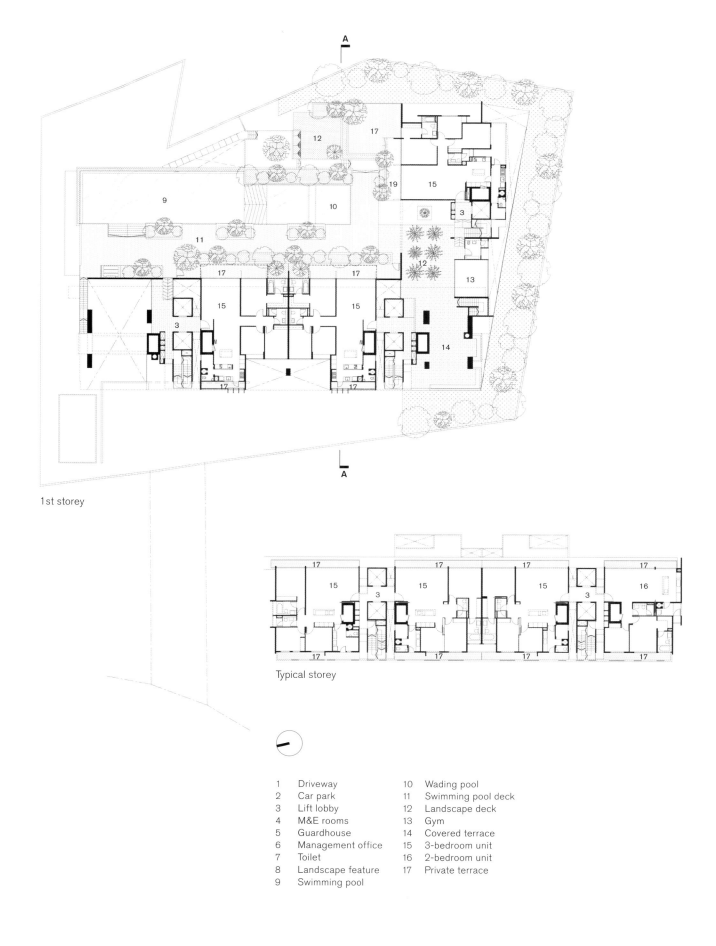

1st storey

Typical storey

1	Driveway	10	Wading pool
2	Car park	11	Swimming pool deck
3	Lift lobby	12	Landscape deck
4	M&E rooms	13	Gym
5	Guardhouse	14	Covered terrace
6	Management office	15	3-bedroom unit
7	Toilet	16	2-bedroom unit
8	Landscape feature	17	Private terrace
9	Swimming pool		

05

West elevation

East elevation

05 Movable sunscreens with framed timber slats.

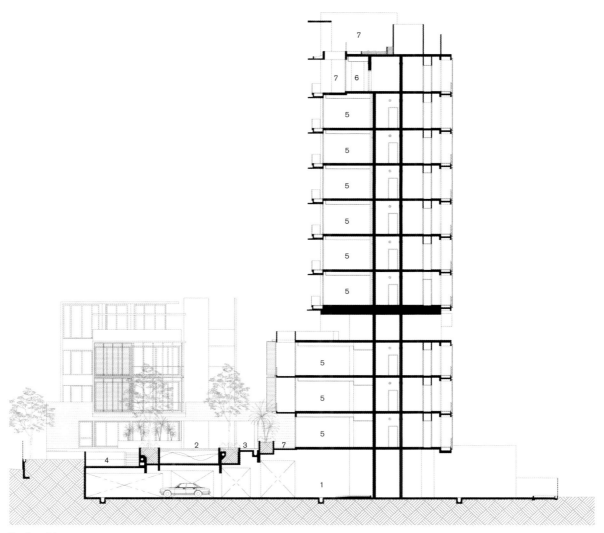

Section AA

1   Car park
2   Swimming pool
3   Swimming pool deck
4   Landscape deck
5   3-bedroom unit
6   5-bedroom unit
7   Private terrace

06 OVERLEAF Three small "houses" at the lower portion of the
development define the lush, inward-looking communal space.

08

07 Unlike the upper slab block, apartments on the lower three storeys are treated like individual houses.

08 A combination of fixed and movable screens adorns the facade of these "houses".

09

10

09 The contrasting lower- and upper-level facades.

10 The clean and linear facade of the slab block.

11 The porous and transparent slab block above the house-like
structures allows the apartments to take in the view beyond.

THE NASSIM

2006–2015

This was our third upmarket housing project in Nassim Hill, one of the most exclusive residential addresses in Singapore. It sits between our work on The Loft (1996–2002) and Tanglin Residences (2002–5). All three developments were restricted by height control, resulting from a prescription by the planning authorities that protects important vistas from within the nearby Singapore Botanic Gardens.

As well as this low-rise requirement, the developer's brief took inspiration from early twentieth-century black and white bungalows. Such housing was popular with the Europeans who stayed here among their spice plantations during the British colonial era. They are characterized by lush greenery and wide verandas on their frontages, and are named after their painted black-and-white facades, which echo the "mock-Tudor" houses of the Victorian era.

Our design captures the essence of such bungalows while offering the facilities of a modern condominium. A key feature of all fifty-five apartments is an expansive balcony that extends the living and dining areas to create covered spaces for social gatherings. While not mimicking their look, this references the black and white bungalows' generous verandas, which maximized cross-ventilation to create a cool part of the home for families to spend time in.

The apartments are housed within eight blocks that surround a landscaped pool area. For the first to third levels of these five-storey blocks, the veranda spaces on the facade are expressed as a series of terraces linked by landscaped bridges. These horizontal decks slide beyond the footprint of the residential blocks to blur the boundaries and building forms. They also enhance the saleable areas, as planning regulations then exempted open-to-sky terraces from the allowable Gross Floor Area calculation. Perched above the landscape decks are units on the fourth and fifth storeys that resemble houses. This massing is enhanced by pitched roofs that conceal the attics of the top-floor apartments. Slatted sliding/folding screens cover their verandas, a reinterpretation of the traditional timber-louvred French windows used in black and white bungalows.

A variety of units is offered in this development, ranging from three-bedroom apartments to five-bedroom duplexes. The larger units also feature private lift lobbies that let residents bypass the social spaces of their apartments and head straight into the private areas. The most exclusive units are the seven penthouses. One even comes with a dedicated lift, a rooftop pool and parking for seven cars – offering the best of both landed housing and apartment living.

01 OPPOSITE Terraces linked by landscaped bridges.

02 Entrance porch to the development.

03 OVERLEAF To reduce the scale of the five-storey development, the first- to third-storey facades are expressed as interconnected landscaped terraces, while the fourth and fifth levels are expressed as "houses" perched on these landscaped decks.

02

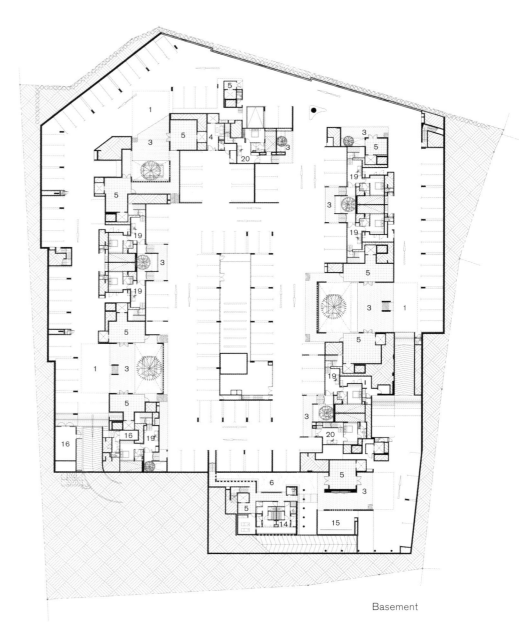

Basement

04

05

04 Sunken courtyards at basement foyers.

05 Reflective pool at entrance to amenities in basement.

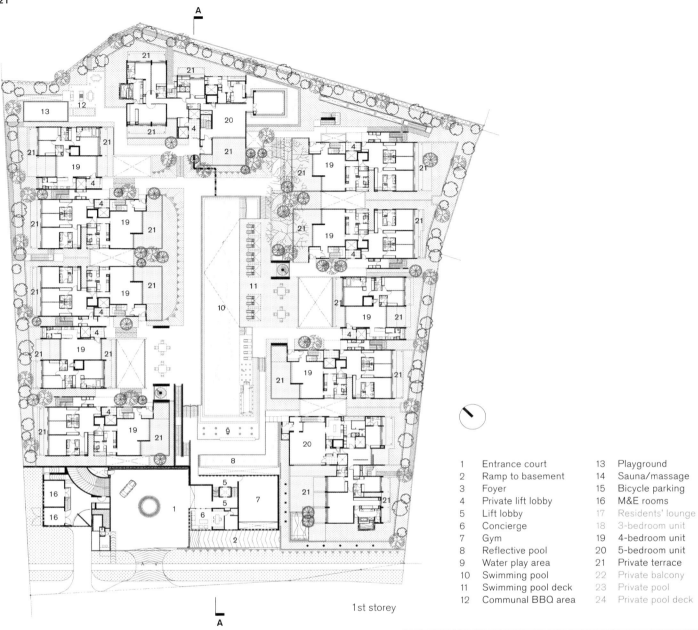

1st storey

1	Entrance court	13	Playground
2	Ramp to basement	14	Sauna/massage
3	Foyer	15	Bicycle parking
4	Private lift lobby	16	M&E rooms
5	Lift lobby	17	Residents' lounge
6	Concierge	18	3-bedroom unit
7	Gym	19	4-bedroom unit
8	Reflective pool	20	5-bedroom unit
9	Water play area	21	Private terrace
10	Swimming pool	22	Private balcony
11	Swimming pool deck	23	Private pool
12	Communal BBQ area	24	Private pool deck

06

06 The roundabout within the entrance porch.

1	Entrance court	13	Playground
2	Ramp to basement	14	Sauna/massage
3	Foyer	15	Bicycle parking
4	Private lift lobby	16	M&E rooms
5	Lift lobby	17	Residents' lounge
6	Concierge	18	3-bedroom unit
7	Gym	19	4-bedroom unit
8	Reflective pool	20	5-bedroom unit
9	Water play area	21	Private terrace
10	Swimming pool	22	Private balcony
11	Swimming pool deck	23	Private pool
12	Communal BBQ area	24	Private pool deck

2nd storey

Section AA

5th storey

Attic storey

07

08

07 & 08 Balconies of the apartments on the upper levels are
shielded with sliding/folding screens.

09

09 Landscaped private terraces on the first three levels.

10

10 A shaded seating area next to the pool.

11 OVERLEAF A lushly landscaped private terrace.

EXTENSION OF PAYA LEBAR METHODIST GIRLS' SECONDARY SCHOOL

2004–2007

For this project, we literally created new ground to overcome the tight site and limited budget. The school required new sports amenities, a six-storey block for teaching facilities and a 750-seat auditorium. However, it sat on a 4-hectare (10-acre) site that was not only smaller than average but was shared with an affiliated institution. This highly congested site was also filled with three classroom blocks, as well as a separate building that housed a canteen and multi-purpose hall.

As the budget ruled out rebuilding the existing block into a single building containing the canteen, the multi-purpose hall and the new amenities, we introduced a "new ground" over the front portion of the original site – the only leftover space for new development. This took the form of a large floor plate lifted up to the third-storey level for the new auditorium and other games courts to sit on. This intervention created space for these programmes, which it would not otherwise have been possible to fit in.

The elevated deck also transforms the school's original ground underneath into a shaded common space, offering much relief in Singapore's tropical climate. The parade square, previously an open-to-sky space, has been transformed into a highly conducive area for students to gather and conduct

school activities such as the daily flag-raising ceremony. To prevent these covered grounds from becoming stifling, they were kept open-sided, while air wells along the perimeter bring in light. In addition, there are large flights of steps and stairways – both open and enclosed – that connect this original ground to the new third storey.

The new ground's organic shape traces the profile of the site. This is in contrast to the rectilinear geometry of the new auditorium, as well as that of the existing block housing the canteen and multi-purpose hall. These two buildings were cladded with inexpensive materials such as metal roofing sheets and plaster over brick. Painstakingly detailed with an economy of means, we transformed them into visual anchors that greet the cars and pedestrians that pass by the school daily.

02

01 OPPOSITE Viewed from the street, the new auditorium (left) and the renovated multi-purpose hall act as visual markers of the school.

02 To overcome the tight site and limited budget, an elevated "new ground" was introduced over the front of the site.

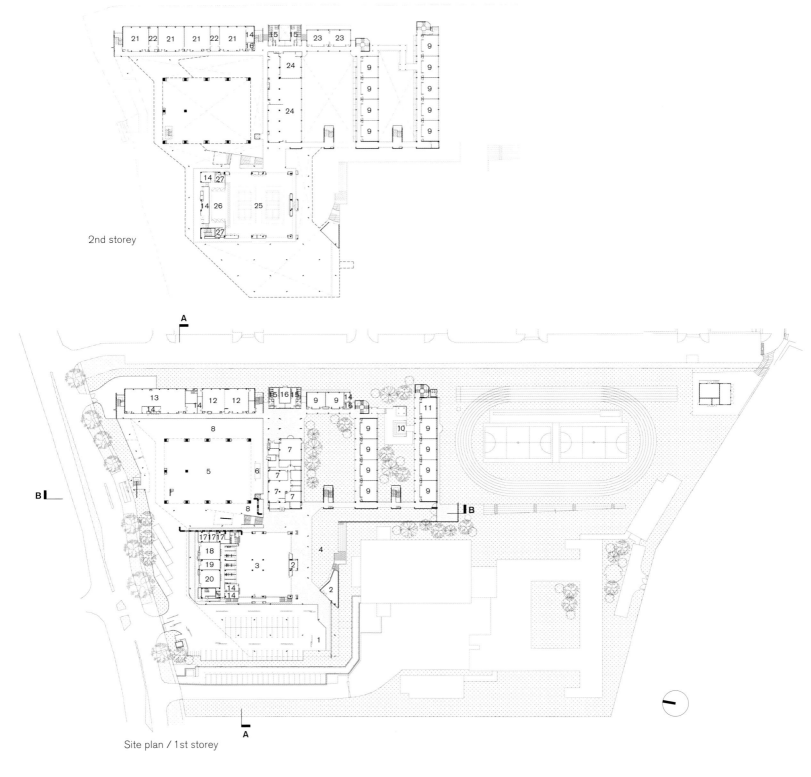

2nd storey

Site plan / 1st storey

1	Drop off	22	Prep store
2	Bookshop	23	Mother-tongue room
3	Canteen	24	Staff area
4	Outdoor performance area	25	Multi-purpose hall
5	Parade square	26	Stage
6	Flag-raising position	27	Changing room
7	Administration office	28	Music room
8	Courtyard	29	Dance studio
9	Classroom	30	IT resource room
10	Covered linkway	31	Library
11	Archive	32	Instructional/computer area
12	Arts and craft	33	Students' activity room
13	Design and technology	34	Prefect room
14	Store	35	Foyer
15	Toilet	36	Auditorium
16	M&E room	37	Outdoor fitness area
17	Function room	38	Basketball court
18	Games-equipment store	39	St John CCA
19	Family education programme room	40	Domestic-science room
20	Health and fitness room	41	Computer lab
21	Laboratory	42	Chapel

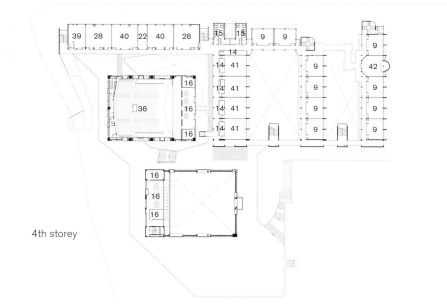

4th storey

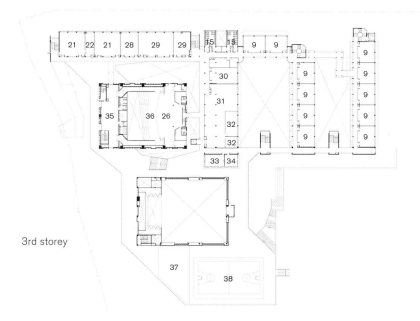

3rd storey

03

03 The elevated deck acts as a shelter for the car park, which would normally be left open to the sky.

04 OVERLEAF The covered parade square is enlivened by perimeter light wells.

05

06

07

05 Large flights of steps and stairways connect the original ground level to the "new ground" at the third level.

06 & 07 The covered parade square offers a conducive environment for activities in the tropical climate.

08 OPPOSITE Arriving at the "new ground".

08

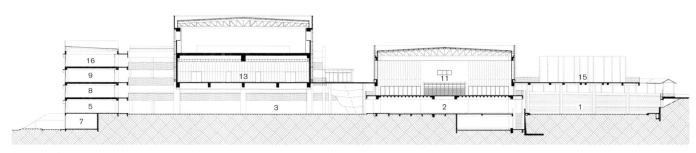

Section AA

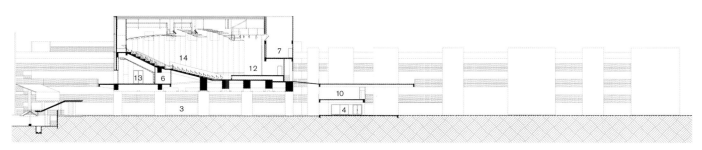

Section BB

1	Drop off	9	Laboratory
2	Canteen	10	Staff area
3	Parade square	11	Multi-purpose hall
4	Administration office	12	Stage
5	Design and technology	13	Foyer
6	Store	14	Auditorium
7	M&E room	15	Outdoor fitness area
8	Function room	16	Domestic-science room

09

10

09 & 10 Facades are detailed with economical materials. On the auditorium facade, plastered walls painted in vertical strips are complemented by adjacent recesses layered with perforated mesh.

11 On the multi-purpose hall, plaster and paint surfaces are juxtaposed with fenestrations formed by corrugated panels.

12 Multi-purpose hall interior.

11

12

SINGAPORE SAFETY DRIVING CENTRE

2006–2009

Facilities for teaching driving and riding usually occupy large tracts of land. Inspired by driving centres in Tokyo, many of which are stacked vertically to reduce their footprint, we proposed this multi-storey driving centre – a first in Singapore.

The centre is located in an industrial area and sits on a rectangular floor plate measuring 170 by 100 metres (560 by 330 feet) – almost the size of two football pitches. Its three levels house separate circuits for different types of vehicles. While the ground floor is for drivers of cars, coaches and trucks to take tests, the second level is a practice circuit for car drivers taking lessons. The third-level rooftop is where motorcyclists take both lessons and tests.

To accommodate the vast layout and provide a functional circuit on all levels, the centre has nine main columns arranged on a grid of 40 by 30 metres (130 by 100 feet). Supporting this are small, shorter-span columns plotted along its periphery. Each main column has extended capitals that support a series of post-tension beams and the floor slab above. On the second storey, these capitals also branch out as a group of four columns to support the rooftop. To bring light and ventilation into the deep floor plate and the lower sections of the centre, we created voids by introducing three linear slits that run parallel to the shorter length of the slab.

The centre's entire second-storey facade was wrapped in a powder-coated wire mesh that also extends above the third-storey perimeter by 2 metres (6½ feet). This safety net breaks the fall of humans – or even vehicles – in the event of an accident. It is held up by the perimeter columns on the second and third levels, which were designed to act as both a series of structural fins and a supporting frame. This tight and economical alignment of form and function was carried through to the exposed services. For example, recessed slots were provided in the post-tension beams to accommodate light fittings.

While the circuits for vehicles run around the entire floor plate, a separate five-storey building was inserted at one end of the centre to house various administrative functions. This building is 80 metres (260 feet) long and 30 metres (100 feet) wide, and has its own small-spanned structural grids. Double-volume spaces were carved out of the block to create a lofty lobby on the first storey, and also a roof garden.

Overall, the aesthetic treatment of this utilitarian building was necessarily an expression of an economy of means. But while each element of the building had to fulfil a functional purpose, every opportunity to infuse delight was seized upon, creating an architecturally coherent building.

01 OPPOSITE Facades wrapped in powder-coated wire mesh, which acts as a safety net.

02 View of the longitudinal facade.

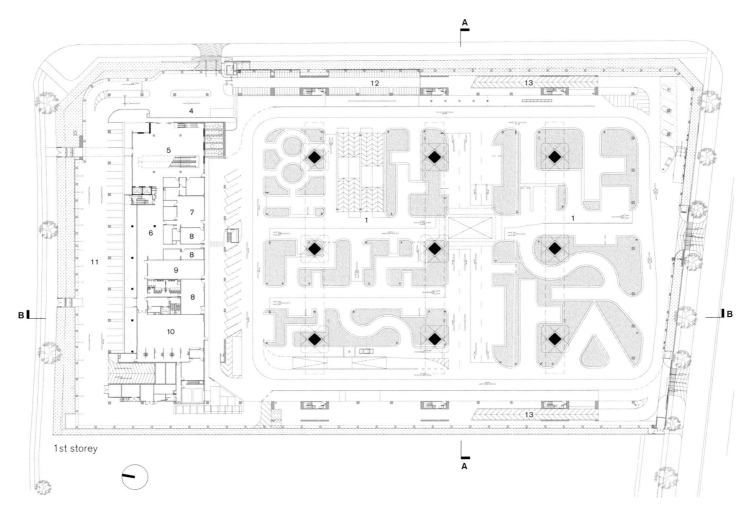

A

A

B

B

1st storey

1   Circuits for driving tests
     (cars/coaches/trucks)
2   Circuits for driving lessons (cars)
3   Circuits for riding lessons and
     tests (motorcycles)
4   Drop off
5   Lobby atrium
6   Waiting area
7   Traffic-police office
8   Test waiting room

9   Theory-test room
10   Canteen
11   Car park
12   Motorcycle park
13   Ramps for cars/motorcycles
14   Office
15   Motorcycle reporting point
16   Staff lounge
17   Staff lockers

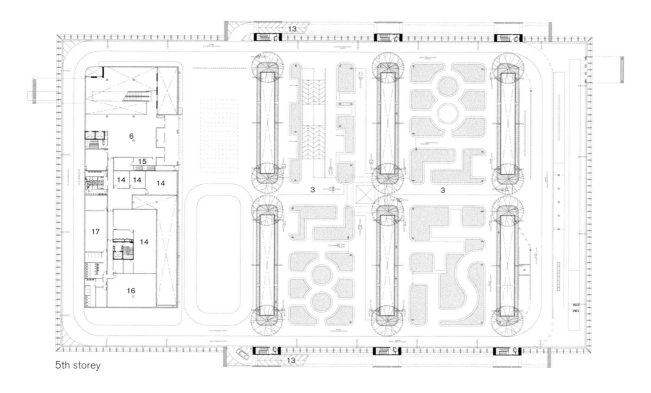

5th storey

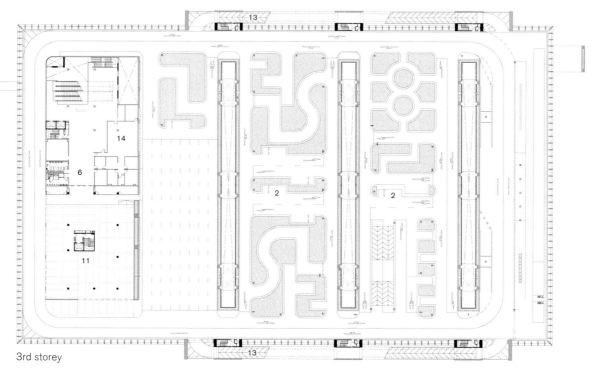

3rd storey

03 OVERLEAF To accommodate the large floor plates with functional circuits on all levels, the building is supported on nine main columns arranged in a 40 by 30m (130 by 100ft) grid.

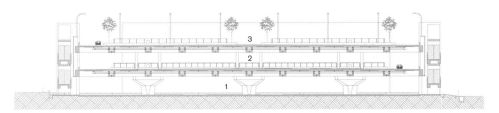

Section AA

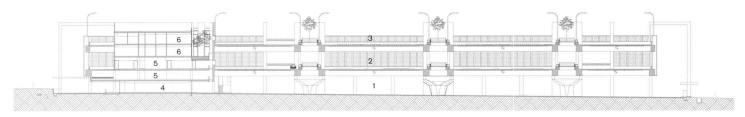

Section BB

04

1   Circuits for driving tests
    (cars/coaches/trucks)
2   Circuits for driving lessons
    (cars)
3   Circuits for riding lessons and
    tests (motorcycles)
4   Canteen
5   Car park
6   Office

04 Linear air wells bring light and ventilation into the deep floor plate.

05 & 06 Various configurations of driving circuits on the first storey.

05

06

07

08

07 A vehicular ramp leading to the rooftop circuits.

08 Second-storey driving circuit. Structural fins on the perimeter double up as supporting frames for the safety nets on the facade.

10

09 & 10 Rooftop riding circuits for motorcyclists.

11 OVERLEAF The vast elevated riding circuits on the rooftop give the impression of an actual streetscape.

THE OLIV

2007–2013

To promote vertical greening in Singapore's increasingly dense built environment, the planning authorities introduced sky terraces in their guidelines in the mid-2000s. This feature is exempted from the all-important Gross Floor Area calculations when used as a communal space, giving developers and architects an incentive to add such vertical landscaping and shared facilities to high-rise developments.

This development is our architectural expression of this planning regulation – pushed to its limits. The twelve-storey condominium consists of front and back blocks served by a spine of common lifts and services. Each block's floor plate has only two units, and they share a 130-square-metre (1,400-square-foot) sky terrace. This stretches the planning authority's idea of such features as communal areas. The 7-metre-high (23-foot-high) sky terraces that front each pair of units look and feel like a private extension. Only a 5-millimetre (³/₁₆-inch) wide diagonal joint line in the deck discreetly divides the shared domain from the private space of each home. The apartments' typical floor plans are configured as duplexes with double-volume living, dining and open kitchen spaces. These align with the balcony and sky terrace outside to form a single integrated space.

The ends of the sky terraces for each level are tapered up or down to prevent users from looking into the bedrooms of the apartments. This gives privacy and creates a dramatic facade. Viewed from the exterior, the sky terraces snake upwards irregularly like a mountain path to the clouds. They are landscaped with abundant tropical foliage, and these extended exteriors serve as large projection canopies that cut off glare from the double-volume interior. The undersides of the organic-shaped terraces are expressed as cast and textured off-form concrete, while their fascias and floors are finished in natural *balau* (a hardwood timber). Such raw and natural qualities contrast sharply with the development's linear geometry.

Instead of seeing rules as restrictions, we demonstrate how they can be used to create new typologies of high-density living in Singapore. Our sky terraces enlarged the idea of what is communal to create a striking building of substantial size, yet with extensive greening. The Oliv takes apartment living to the next level to create "bungalows in the air".

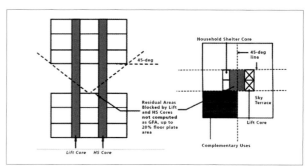

02

01 **OPPOSITE** The organic, textured, off-form planters juxtaposed with the sleek aluminium screens.

02 Diagram illustrating the concept of the residual Gross Floor Area exemption.

03

04

03 Sky terraces on the north and south facades.

04 Movable sunscreens on the east and west facades.

05 The facade is made up of a series of undulating sky terraces.

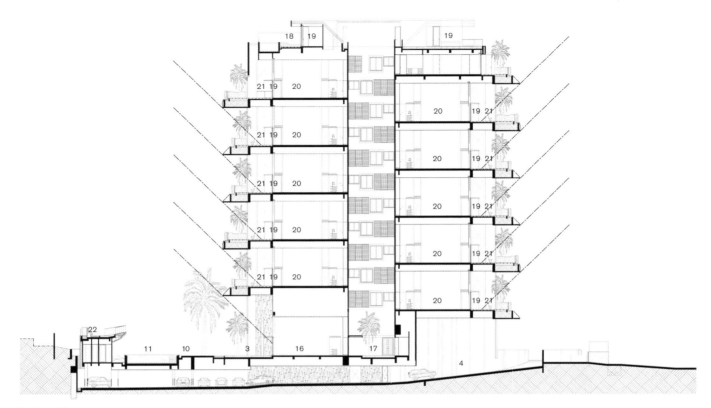

Section AA

06   07

06 The entrance court.

07 A stone-clad corridor leading from the drop-off porch to facilities at the rear.

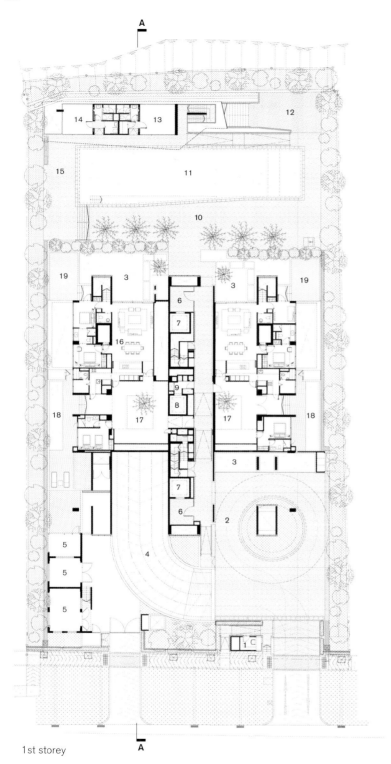

1st storey

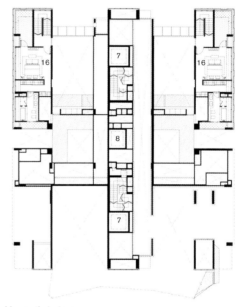

Upper 1st storey

1	Guardhouse	12	Playground
2	Entrance court	13	Gym
3	Water feature	14	Function room
4	Ramp to basement car park	15	BBQ area
5	Substation	16	Ground-floor duplex
6	Passenger lift lobby	17	Private decorative pond
7	Passenger lift	18	Private cross-current pool
8	Service lift	19	Private terrace
9	Service lift lobby	20	Upper-level duplex
10	Pool deck	21	Sky terrace
11	Lap pool	22	Roof terrace

09

08 OPPOSITE View of the pool and the clubhouse, with green
wall on folded slab in the foreground.

09 A connecting stairway brings light into the basement.

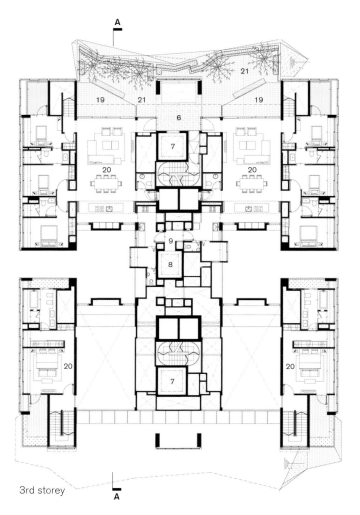

3rd storey

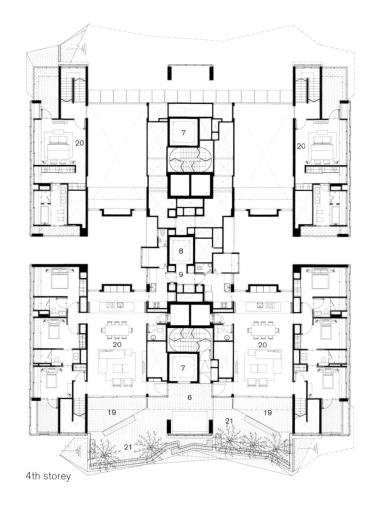

4th storey

1	Guardhouse	12	Playground
2	Entrance court	13	Gym
3	Water feature	14	Function room
4	Ramp to basement car park	15	BBQ area
5	Substation	16	Ground-floor duplex
6	Passenger lift lobby	17	Private decorative pond
7	Passenger lift	18	Private cross-current pool
8	Service lift	19	Private terrace
9	Service lift lobby	20	Upper-level duplex
10	Pool deck	21	Sky terrace
11	Lap pool	22	Roof terrace

10

11

10 Water feature at the lift lobby.

11 Seamless connection between the private balcony and the communal sky terrace.

12 OVERLEAF The double-volume interior space aligns with the balcony and sky terrace outside to form an integral spatial continuum.

THE PARTY HOUSE

2007–2012

From the Villa Savoye by Le Corbusier to the Glass House by Philip Johnson, many of the great modern houses are country retreats that were not designed primarily for living. The Party House was such a commission, as the client wanted a home to entertain and impress. This two-storey detached house located in Sentosa Cove – Singapore's expensive oceanfront development – achieves this aim subtly with a muted structure cloaked by a mysterious mesh, which hides a sensual playground inside.

With the entertainment function in mind, the bedrooms are placed in the basement, but are relieved with sunken landscaped light wells. Arising from this is a sequence that progressively takes guests through different moods, all the way to a rooftop pool. The journey begins with a descent into a double-volume basement, an experience akin to entering an underground bar in New York. Inside this cavernous, chiselled, off-form concrete shell, guests have pre-dinner drinks and then head up to the first floor for an intimate meal. Above this level, a glossy world of refined surfaces awaits. The second floor is laid out in polished black floors and sleek metal ceilings, and houses a series of activity rooms – a men's club, a karaoke lounge and a winter-themed room for the ladies complete with a working fireplace – that seemingly float in space like jewel boxes. These are enclosed by glass partitions, which can be neatly stashed away to open up the entire floor, allowing large parties to be hosted too.

Lining the house's entire second storey is a veranda wrapped by a subtle mesh curtain. This delicate backdrop is in constant dialogue with the environment, softly echoing the changing colour of the sun throughout the day and dancing in the breeze like a large-scale wind chime. Such an expressive feature actually arose out of very practical concerns. A movable screen allowed us to avoid incurring additional Gross Floor Area for a plot of land that had a very strict cap.

We originally proposed a movable metal screen with floral cut-outs, but struggled with such a clumsy and ubiquitous solution. Midway through construction, the idea of a mesh came about – obliquely referencing the flowy curtains found in Shigeru Ban's Curtain Wall House. Like a veil, the sheer mesh gently screens the house from its neighbours, while offering guests a magical scene with views to the sea. The feature gives The Party House an ethereal quality and its own unique signature.

01 The house is a muted concrete structure cloaked by a stainless-steel curtain.

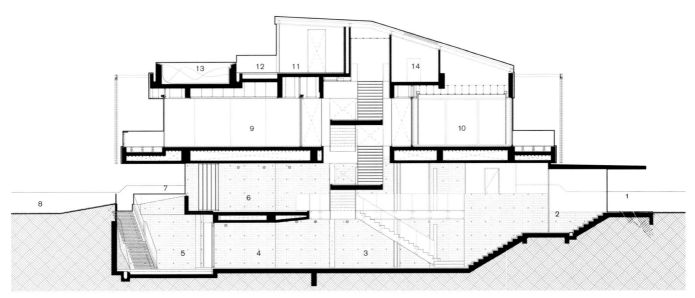

Section AA

1	Car porch	8	Garden
2	Entrance	9	Men's club
3	Pre-dining area	10	Karaoke room
4	Bar	11	Summer room
5	Water feature	12	Pool deck
6	Dining area	13	Swimming pool
7	Patio	14	M&E services

02 Stairway leading to a double-volume basement space, containing an area for pre-dinner drinks.

02

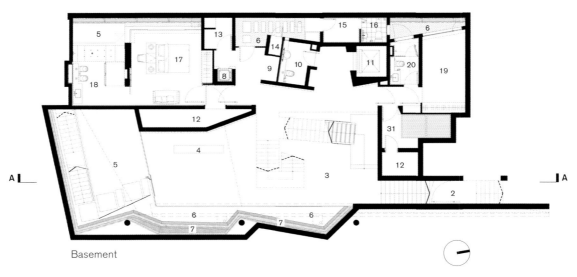

Basement

1	Car porch	12	Store	23	Garden
2	Entrance	13	Server room	24	Kitchen
3	Pre-dining area	14	Pump room	25	Men's club
4	Bar	15	Maid's room	26	Winter room
5	Water feature	16	Maid's toilet	27	Karaoke room
6	Courtyard	17	Master bedroom	28	Summer room
7	Green wall	18	Master bathroom	29	Pool deck
8	Dumb waiter	19	Guest room	30	Swimming pool
9	Servery	20	Guest bathroom	31	M&E services
10	Powder room	21	Dining area		
11	Lift	22	Patio		

03

03 Landscaped light wells provide relief in the basement space.

04 OPPOSITE A cavernous off-form concrete shell housing the pre-dinner drinks space, with a view to the formal dining above.

06

1st storey

05 An open stairway connects the
basement and the formal dining area.

06 Formal dining area with view of the sea.

1	Car porch	12	Store	23	Garden
2	Entrance	13	Server room	24	Kitchen
3	Pre-dining area	14	Pump room	25	Men's club
4	Bar	15	Maid's room	26	Winter room
5	Water feature	16	Maid's toilet	27	Karaoke room
6	Courtyard	17	Master bedroom	28	Summer room
7	Green wall	18	Master bathroom	29	Pool deck
8	Dumb waiter	19	Guest room	30	Swimming pool
9	Servery	20	Guest bathroom	31	M&E services
10	Powder room	21	Dining area		
11	Lift	22	Patio		

07

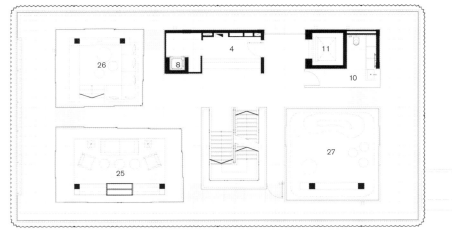

2nd storey

07 & 08 Arriving at the second floor, which contains a series of after-dinner activity rooms in a glossy world of reflective finishes.

08

09 OVERLEAF The men's club (left) and the winter-themed room for the ladies (right) are akin to jewel boxes floating in space, with the undulating mesh curtain providing a sensual backdrop.

10

11

12

13

10, 11, 12 & 13 Like a veil, the mesh curtain gently screens
The Party House from the neighbourhood while offering guests
a view to the sea.

14

14 The rooftop pool overlooking the sea.

15 The house animated by internal lighting after dark.

EDUCATION RESOURCE CENTRE

2008–2011

Located in the heart of the National University of Singapore's new University Town (UTown), this two-storey building was designed for students and researchers to work and learn together. The multi-programmed facility offers a 200-seat auditorium, study clusters, a learning café and multiple seminar rooms. These are deliberately housed in a low-rise building so as not to compete with the towering residential colleges that surround it. Instead, we topped the centre with a large green roof that not only seems to double the greenery of the neighbouring lawn, the Town Green, but also offers occupants of the nearby high-rise buildings a fifth elevation to look down on.

The shape of the building takes advantage of the topography of the 10,000-square-metre (108,000-square-foot) site, a former golf course filled with many beautiful mature trees. The first-storey floor plate is fully integrated with the site, which gently slopes from its rear to the Town Green in front. This helps to conserve the existing trees, including several magnificent 25-metre-tall (82-foot-tall) tembusus that have been turned into strategic markers at the centre's entrance and in its central courtyard. The large floor plates also support the centre in enabling collaborative learning communities. They offer flexibility in placing amenities so as to facilitate interaction and maximize visual connection.

Connecting the organic-shaped floor plates at various levels are gentle ramps that surround the central courtyard or are distributed along the building's perimeter. This arrangement offers a progressive spatial experience as visitors move from the northern entrance through to the courtyard and study platforms in the middle. Arriving at the open-sided foyer in the south, they are greeted by a wide and elevated view of the Town Green as well as a double-volume covered study area below. The gentle breeze that frequently flows through this open-sided space makes it one of UTown's most popular spots to hang out.

The centre's spaces are naturally ventilated wherever possible. This include its large foyer, lift lobbies, circulation paths and some thirty per cent of the study areas. A large courtyard also punctuates the floor plates to draw cool air down and induce natural breezes. In addition, the centre's major entrances and facade openings are oriented in the north–south direction to ensure cross-ventilation within.

A key architectural feature is an 8.5-metre-tall (28-foot-tall) pigmented fair-faced concrete wall that encloses the auditorium. This faces the Town Green and was individually cast layer by layer using five batches of concrete mixes, which had varying amounts of red and grey pigment added into white cement. The resulting undulating surface is distinctive, and especially striking when it is lit up at night.

01 OPPOSITE A porous tropical building.

02 OVERLEAF The large green roof of the low-rise building perceptibly doubles the size of the Town Green it faces, offering occupants of the neighbouring high-rise towers a fifth elevation to view.

C

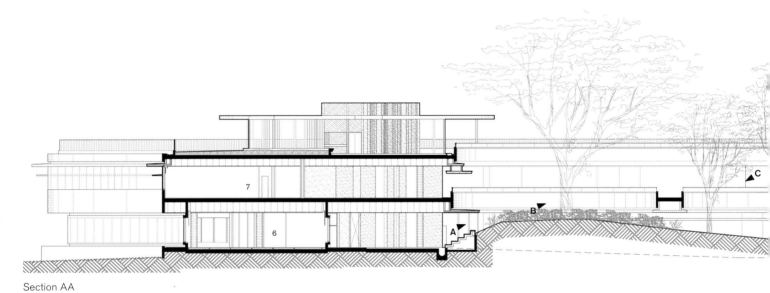

Section AA

A

B

1   Covered study area
2   Indoor learning café
3   Town Green
4   Foyer
5   Courtyard
6   PC commons
7   Seminar room

D

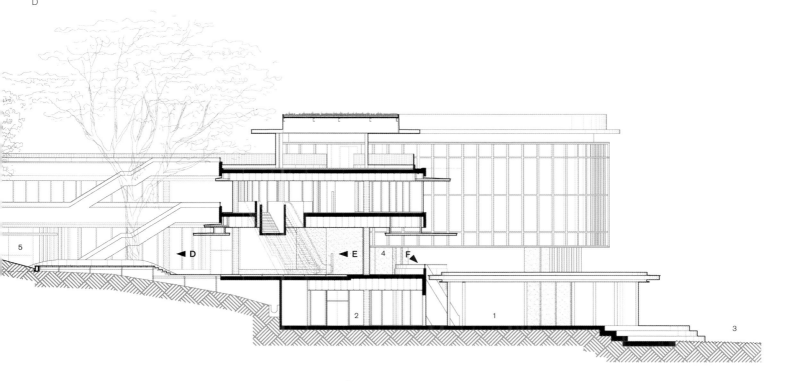

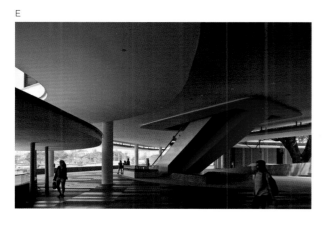

E

F

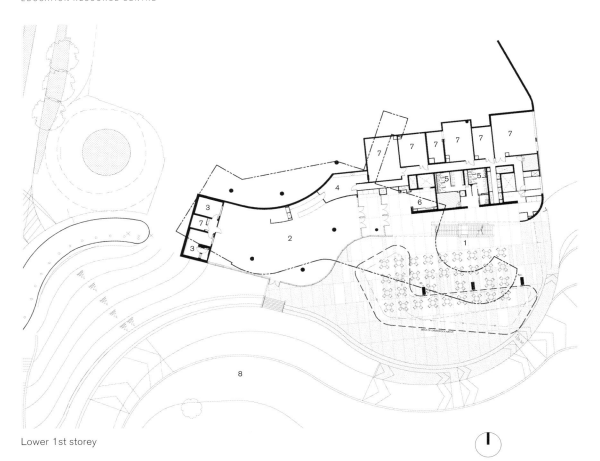

Lower 1st storey

04

1	Covered study area	18	ERC staff and
2	Indoor learning café		student office
3	Broadcast console	19	Mac commons
4	Food prep and wash bay	20	Store
5	Toilet	21	Open study area
6	Lift lobby	22	Seminar room
7	M&E rooms	23	Smart classroom
8	Town Green	24	Problem-based
9	Drop off		learning class
10	Foyer	25	Faculty lounge
11	Courtyard	26	Writing-unit office
12	Collaborative commons	27	Auditorium lobby
13	PC commons	28	Auditorium
14	Meeting room	29	Private study cluster
15	Visualization suite	30	VIP lounge
16	Conference suite	31	Roof terrace
17	Presentation space		

03 PREVIOUS Gentle ramps surround the central courtyard, where mature conserved trees reside.

04 A double-volume, naturally ventilated study area overlooks the Town Green.

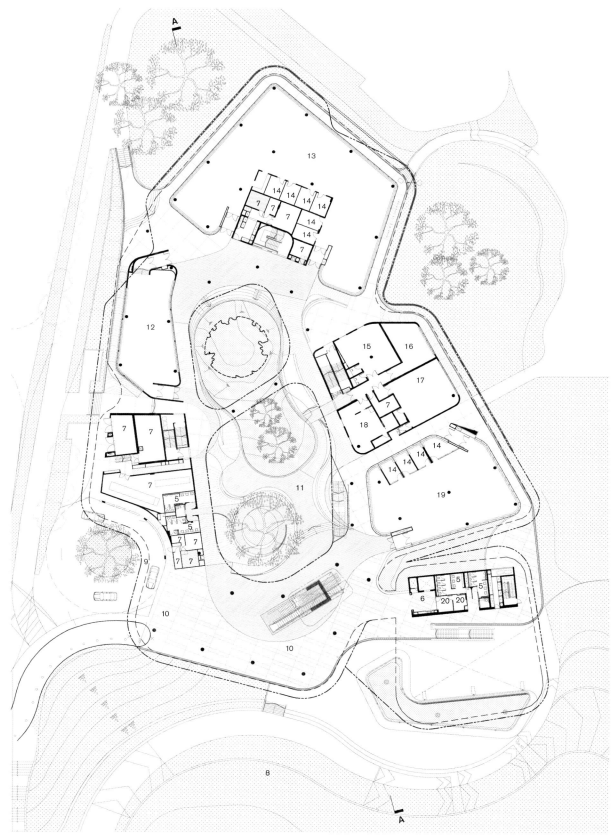

1st storey

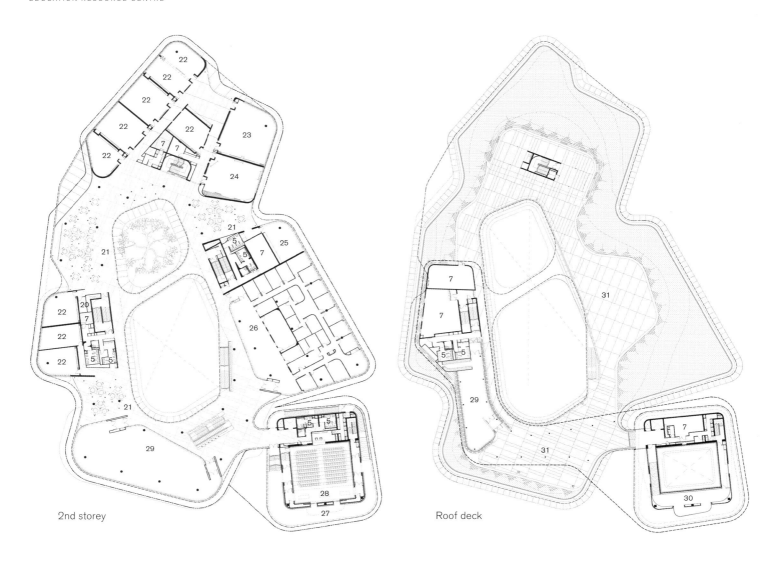

2nd storey

Roof deck

1	Covered study area	18	ERC staff and
2	Indoor learning café		student office
3	Broadcast console	19	Mac commons
4	Food prep and wash bay	20	Store
5	Toilet	21	Open study area
6	Lift lobby	22	Seminar room
7	M&E rooms	23	Smart classroom
8	Town Green	24	Problem-based
9	Drop off		learning class
10	Foyer	25	Faculty lounge
11	Courtyard	26	Writing-unit office
12	Collaborative commons	27	Auditorium lobby
13	PC commons	28	Auditorium
14	Meeting room	29	Private study cluster
15	Visualization suite	30	VIP lounge
16	Conference suite	31	Roof terrace
17	Presentation space		

05

06

07

05 Naturally ventilated spaces complement the air-conditioned study areas.

06 & 07 Large horizontal fins that adorn the facades act as sun and rain screens.

09

08 A pigmented fair-faced concrete wall encloses the auditorium.

09 Recycled-timber slats clad the interior acoustic walls of the auditorium.

10 OVERLEAF View of the building from the Town Green.

11 KIM TIAN ROAD

2013–2018

A distinctive elevated communal deck links these three apartment blocks while also relating the residential development to its historic neighbours. This feature was introduced to overcome the challenges of a site divided into two disconnected chunks – a consequence of a no-build strip that the planning authorities had mandated to protect views of the surrounding residences. These include a series of four-storey Singapore Improvement Trust (SIT) flats within the Tiong Bahru estate, one of the city's first public-housing estates.

The deck is finished in off-form concrete and rises five storeys above ground to string together various communal spaces, including barbecue pavilions, landscaped gardens and outdoor lounges. The twisted undulating strip conveys a sense of fluidity but also subtly keeps people from looking over into the units below. Instead, it offers views of the swimming pools and children's playground on the ground, and is connected to the main entrance by a bridge that wraps around the southernmost tower.

In addition to the no-build strip, the planning authorities originally stipulated that the three towers in the development should step down as they recede from the main thoroughfare, Tiong Bahru Road. We successfully proposed a different interpretation. To create greater unity, we designed a pair of thirty-six-storey towers instead. These line up almost exactly with the existing SIT flats lining Lim Liak Street, forming a symmetrical anchor to the Tiong Bahru estate. Each tower is topped with suites for hosting events and offers panoramic views of the surroundings.

On the other side of the no-build strip sits a significantly shorter third tower. This features large cut-outs that contain sky terraces, one of which even has a gym. These terraces are framed by brackets of off-form concrete to create a link with the elevated deck. While the tower stands apart from the rest of the development, it not only acknowledges a small public park just below but also serves as an anchor addressing the approach from Kim Tian Road.

01

01 The vantage point from the top of the twin towers offers a view of the city.

02 OPPOSITE Flanked by low-rise housing blocks, the twin towers anchor the vista from Lim Liak Street.

03

TOWER A   TOWER B

TOWER C

ELEVATED COMMUNAL DECK

TIONG BAHRU
ROAD

West elevation

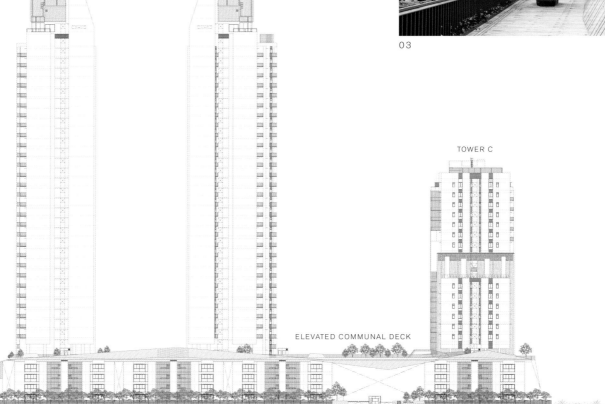

04

03 Tower C seen from the elevated communal deck.
04 Tower C offers a focal point from an approaching road.

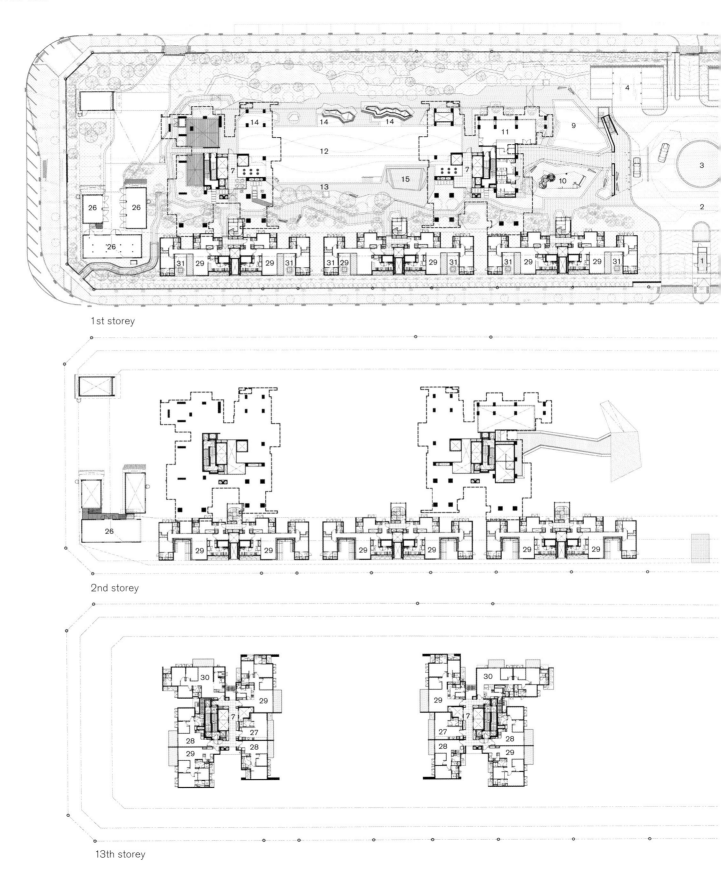

1st storey

2nd storey

13th storey

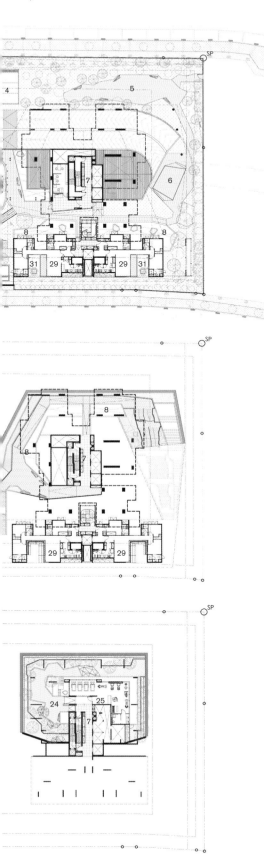

05

06

1	Guardhouse	17	Swing garden
2	Arrival plaza	18	Fitness pavilion
3	Landscape feature	19	Reflexology walk
4	Open car park	20	Art lounge
5	Garden deck	21	Elevated landscape deck
6	BBQ pavilion	22	Butterfly garden
7	Lift lobby	23	Aqua spring
8	Water feature	24	Sky terrace
9	Children's pool	25	Gym
10	Children's playground	26	M&E rooms
11	Clubhouse	27	1-bedroom unit
12	Swimming pool	28	2-bedroom unit
13	Swimming pool deck	29	3-bedroom unit
14	Aqua deck	30	4-bedroom unit
15	Pool pavilion	31	Water courtyard
16	Dream-catcher garden		

05 A view corridor across the development.

06 The arrival plaza.

A

B

Elevated communal deck

H

G

C

D

1 Guardhouse	17 Swing garden
2 Arrival plaza	18 Fitness pavilion
3 Landscape feature	19 Reflexology walk
4 Open car park	20 Art lounge
5 Garden deck	21 Elevated landscape deck
6 BBQ pavilion	22 Butterfly garden
7 Lift lobby	23 Aqua spring
8 Water feature	24 Sky terrace
9 Children's pool	25 Gym
10 Children's playground	26 M&E rooms
11 Clubhouse	27 1-bedroom unit
12 Swimming pool	28 2-bedroom unit
13 Swimming pool deck	29 3-bedroom unit
14 Aqua deck	30 4-bedroom unit
15 Pool pavilion	31 Water courtyard
16 Dream-catcher garden	

E

F

07 OVERLEAF The high-rise development is set within one of the city's first public-housing estates.

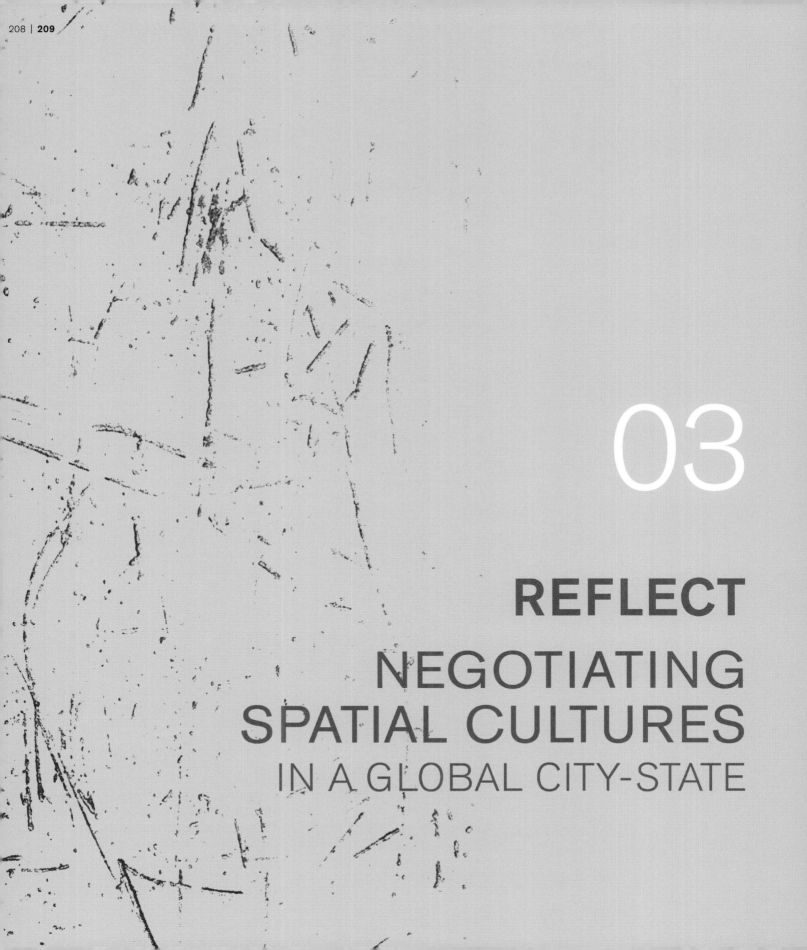

03

REFLECT
NEGOTIATING
SPATIAL CULTURES
IN A GLOBAL CITY-STATE

FIGS. 1 & 2 *Chinese More or Less* exhibition at the Aedes Gallery, Berlin, 2006.

FIG. 3 Catalogue of the exhibition.

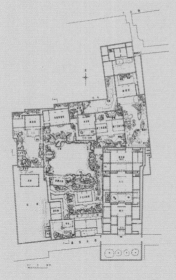

FIG. 4 Plan of the Master of the Nets Garden: the ordered sequence of spaces in the quarters contrasts with the organic layout of the garden.

1 This title was originally conceived by award-winning writer Lynn Pan for a 1998 exhibition on overseas Chinese that I designed for the Chinese Heritage Centre at Nanyang Technological University. With her permission, I subsequently adopted this name for our exhibition and its catalogue.

2 I am not alone in imagining the intricacies of the spaces described in this book. While working on its English translation, Oxford don David Hawkes made multiple attempts to sketch the plans of the great house based on the book's descriptions in order to reconstruct and understand the movements of the people that lived there. These handwritten notes were published in *The Story of the Stone: A Translator's Notebooks* (Hong Kong: Centre for Literature and Translation, Lingnan University, 2000).

In this age of globalization, to speak of one's identity as being rooted in a sense of place seems almost myopic. Yet, without a sense of self, how does one sustain engagement with a world that has increasingly fluid boundaries and intensified exchanges? This struggle is particularly pertinent for artists and architects in a migrant society such as Singapore.

I first made this observation in 2006 when W Architects staged *Chinese More or Less*, an exhibition of our works at the Aedes Gallery, Berlin.[1] FIGS. 1 & 2 In the accompanying catalogue, I recorded a dialogue with architecture critic Leon van Schaik and sociologist Kwok Kian Woon on the cultural undertones in our works. FIG. 3 In the course of working on this monograph, I found myself referring to this past discussion often, and I will build upon it here by referencing a larger body of our works.

Singapore is a child of globalization from its beginning as a trading centre in the Malay Archipelago and later as a colonial port-city. After freeing itself from colonial rule as a part of the Federation of Malaysia in 1963, it then experienced a sudden separation in 1965 to become an independent nation-state. This condition has shaped the mindset of Singapore "to survive by embracing 'the world as our hinterland' and pursuing fast-paced modernization", said Kwok. He went on to quote one of Singapore's foremost playwrights, the late Kuo Pao Kun, who eloquently identified its citizens as "cultural orphans":

> Singaporeans sense the richness of interacting with every place but feel the pain and frustration of not belonging anywhere. Boundless space, boundless bewilderment, boundless loss, boundless hope – there naturally emerges a condition of marginality. Even if we were able to trace back and return to our own respective cultural parentages, we would still not be at home in the past. The orphan can only grope for a way forward, to make his home in the midst of loss and alienation.

According to Kwok, Kuo did not see such cultural homelessness as a negative condition. Instead, it encourages a deeper and more intense search for identity. My own cultural condition can be said to be "overwhelmingly" Chinese in Singapore's multicultural society. Besides being an ethnic Chinese, I was schooled in Chinese-language schools for twelve years up to pre-university level, and my family had a greater than usual exposure to Chinese literature and the arts. However, as Kwok then pointed out, "there are different kinds of Chinese and Chinese-ness in Singapore". For example, compared to migrants from China, the Peranakan Chinese, who have lived for several generations in Southeast Asia, are less oriented towards China and its great traditions. In addition, Singapore's school system under colonial rule allowed for the language of instruction to be either in English or Chinese, and this created a "great divide" in our society that persists till today.

I was among the last cohort of students to be schooled in Chinese before the national curriculum turned bilingual, with English as the main medium of instruction. As English became the dominant language after Singapore's independence, Kwok also observed that the Chinese-educated here "have had to face challenges in becoming part of the mainstream and also in engaging deeply with their tradition". Indeed, one might say that the cessation of the Chinese-language schools in Singapore during the late 1970s was not unlike a mini-Cultural Revolution that further marginalized the Chinese-educated. Thus, while there is richness and joy growing up in multicultural Singapore, there is also the condition of cultural loss and dislocation that has been, and continues to be, experienced by a segment of the society, and this is a condition that I can identify with.

On reflection, my exposure to Chinese literary and aesthetic values in my youth has been a rich cultural resource that I often draw from. In the dialogue mentioned above, van Schaik spoke of how we are all born into "specific rooms in specific places" and we have to draw out a "spatial intelligence" that "we have learned and locked away deep within us". While I cannot recall real physical environments that had a great impact on me while growing up, I do hold within me certain spatial imagery built up over the years through my exposure to Chinese literature, such as *The Story of the Stone*. This great classic by Cao Xueqin (曹雪芹) from the late Qing period captures the author's philosophical outlook, and is narrated through the life of a great family at its height and eventual fall. The nuanced descriptions of day-to-day living serve up a feast for all senses, from the celebratory events marked with particular rituals and customs; the materials and colours of clothing and adornments worn from head to toe; the food served in different seasons for various occasions; and, above all, the tale's exquisite setting in a classical Chinese garden. This garden was described as being in the style of those built south of the Yangtze River, which characteristically embodied all the aesthetic and cultural sensibilities of the Chinese literati.

Reading this great classic created a vivid sense of space in my mindscape, such that I felt as if I knew the spaces intimately and could even imagine navigating my way through the grounds.[2] Ironically, I did not visit a real classical garden until 1988, some six years after working on my thesis project, the Chinatown Infill (1981–82). The garden that left the most vivid impression on me during this trip was the Master of the Nets Garden (网师园) in Suzhou, which was subsequently gazetted as a UNESCO World Heritage Site in 1997. [FIG. 4] As I walked through the garden, it was a particularly absorbing experience to match the wellspring of images in my mind and the actual spatial sequences. This was further enhanced by observing how the domestic quarters and the garden came together as a whole. While not captured in the novel, the intriguing contrast between the ordered sequences of the residential spaces and the picturesque, organic design of the garden gave the entire experience an added spatial dimension. These experiences led me to distil the spatial quality of Chinese gardens in these words:

> A world of rich spatiality is defined inwardly and concealed by boundary walls that project an understated outward image; the richness of spaces within are connected by choreographed routes, which heighten the aesthetic and sensual experience. Experienced in their totality, the ordered spatial sequence of the living quarters and the organic picturesque quality of the garden embody a sense of dualism that holds in harmony elements of contrasting natures, which very much reflects the Chinese outlook on life.

Architecture as Cultural Translation

One of the pitfalls of trying to turn a tradition into a contemporary architectural expression is ending up with a mere literal representation. In our dialogue, Kwok had then emphasized the importance of "translating tradition", and he elaborated on the need for "cultural knowledge of past and present to build a bridge across time and space". Thus, it is not about making direct references by incorporating symbols of the tradition, but synthesizing it with new contexts and with different impetuses. In retrospect, this has taken place in many of our projects.

In Chinatown Infill, the ideal of a Chinese garden space was translated into a dense urban context, with the shophouses acting as the "boundary wall" that concealed the courtyard space within. The essence of this project was to create varied experiential journeys from the streets to the courtyard on a compact scale,

FIG. 5 A model of the Chinatown Infill project (1981–82) with the shophouses acting as "boundary walls" concealing the courtyard space within.

FIG. 6 At the Tampines North Community Centre (1986–89), fragmented massings are contained within a "circulation frame".

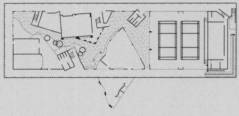

FIG. 7 The circulation frame defines the building's facades.

FIG. 8 Behind the facades, courtyards and alleyways are interspersed between fragmented building blocks.

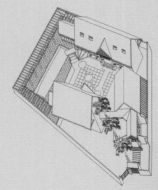

FIG. 9 Chee's House (1983) was an early exploration in using fragmented blocks to form a single house.

FIG. 10 Reuters House (1988) was the first built example of a tropical home with a fragmented massing.

and to evoke the picturesque quality of a "garden" in the condensed space. FIG. 5 The Tampines North Community Centre (1986–89) can also be read as a series of efforts to translate a global influence – Frank Gehry's Postmodernism – into local conditions. The fragmentation of the massing in the community centre resulted in a series of buildings, and gave rise to courtyards, alleys and residual open-to-sky spaces in between them. FIG. 6 Our strategy of tying these disparate entities and spaces together with a two-storey-high circulation corridor both formed the main facade of the building and concealed the rich array of spaces within, which were revealed only when one walked through them. FIG. 7 Herein lies the departure from Gehry. Instead of focusing on the fragmented blocks as distinctive forms, a decision was made to accentuate the resulting in-between spaces. FIG. 8

This strategy of fragmented massing was subsequently translated into a series of housing projects that formed the basis of what is now known as the "tropical bungalow" typology in Southeast Asia. By fragmenting and breaking up a house, we could articulate it as a series of structures within a compound, surrounded by open spaces. This blurred the boundaries between nature and the indoors, and enhanced the views towards the exteriors. The residual spaces also allowed activities to flow unabated between indoors and outdoors. Fragmentation was also used to address other issues, such as climate and culture. Having initially adopted a global – and what some may call Postmodern – reference point, it is interesting to see, in retrospect, that we arrived at a spatial typology that in fact greatly resembles traditional houses found in Asia. However, the spatial quality of the tropical bungalow typology was responsive to climate but was not culturally specific. For instance, in similar typologies of houses in China or Japan, the relationships of the free-standing structures and the open spaces are arranged to reflect specific aesthetic values. In the case of Balinese houses, this is according to religious and cosmic values. In contrast, our tropical bungalows were like blank canvases, capable of receiving different cultural values.

The first of the tropical bungalows I designed with William Lim was Chee's House (1983), which remained unbuilt because the fragmented massing, which almost resembled a traditional *kampong* (Malay village) house, was too far removed from the client's idea of a unified grand villa. FIG. 9 In 1988, Lim's second attempt to design such a house, this time for the Reuters news agency, was successfully carried out. The dominant form of the house was based on the traditional pitched roof, finished with clay tiles. However, the plan, with its bedroom wing pivoted away from the main house to create a garden with a lap pool in the open space in between, adopted the same strategy of fragmentation prevalent in many of our projects at the time. FIG. 10 Lim subsequently designed many such bungalows that combined fragmented plans with traditional forms, and he would later coin the term "Contemporary Vernacular" to describe this stylistic expression.[3]

While my Morley Road House (1996–99) was based on the tropical bungalow typology, I assembled the spaces to meet the client's desire to reflect his Chinese identity. The process of translation was about creating a "Chinese garden" that was within the framework of building guidelines and also suitable for the tropical climate. A series of small gardens along a choreographed route was carved out of spaces between the boundary walls and the building setbacks, a necessity to promote ventilation in the hot and humid tropical climate. FIG. 11 Along this route, views were strategically concealed FIG. 12 and deliberately revealed to orchestrate the climax of viewing the main garden at the end of the journey. FIG. 13 The house was also a significant departure from Lim's Contemporary Vernacular style as it used a Neomodernist expression similar to Lem's House II (1995–97). As van Schaik described it in his review of the house for *Singapore Architect*, this was an "uncompromisingly modern building [that] grew organically from the classical tradition that it is embedded in".[4]

In 2004, we embarked on yet another process of translation when we designed the Beijing House as part of a project initiated by the respected Chinese architect Chang Yung Ho (张永和) to showcase the work of Chinese and overseas Chinese architects. In each of the plots of land that Chang tasked an architect to design, he set a different configuration of 4-metre (13-foot) walls. FIG. 14 We responded to Chang's ideogram with a house of contrasting elements: inward-looking versus outward-facing, as well as enclosed versus open spaces. FIG. 15 This time, we transported the tropicalized Chinese garden concept of Morley Road House back to Beijing, a city filled with hutongs and courtyard houses. Without the requirement of building setbacks between the properties, the footprint of the house was extended to the boundaries. FIG. 16 Within the inward-looking walls of the house, a series of cellular and courtyard spaces was created in a chessboard-like layout. Beyond the confines of the walls, a free-standing pavilion structure was positioned to look out to the

FIG. 11 Porous, tropical spaces are assembled to evoke the spatial quality of a Chinese garden in the Morley Road House (1996–99).

FIG. 12 Garden walls are strategically employed to conceal and reveal spaces.

FIG. 13 The main garden at the Morley Road House.

FIG. 14 Chang Yung Ho's 2004 master plan for the development of twelve houses in Beijing, each inscribed with an ideogram in the form of a continuous wall.

FIG. 16 Model of the Beijing House.

 THE GENESIS

 ENCLOSED
OPEN

 DUAL SPACES

 院落 DWELLING – CELLULAR
园林 GARDEN – OPEN PAVILION

 THE SCENIC ROUTE

 HOUSE FOR ENTERTAINMENT/
HOUSE FOR PRIVATE LIVING

FIG. 15 Contrasting elements in the Beijing House (2004) are conceptualized as a response to the ideogram.

3 See William S. W. Lim and Tan Hock Beng, *Contemporary Vernacular: Evoking Traditions in Asian Architecture* (Singapore: Select Publishing, 1998).

4 See "Between Abstraction and Cultural Reference: House at Morley Road", *Singapore Architect*, no. 201, 1999, pp. 24–31.

FIG. 17 A set of Peranakan gilded screens was incorporated into the design of Goh's House (1982–84).

FIG. 18 A taut glass wall wraps around the entire restaurant space at Da Paolo e Judie (1999–2001), creating reflective surfaces while accentuating conserved elements.

FIG. 19 Colonial buildings occupy the northern bank of the Singapore River, c. 1988–90.

garden, thus transporting a Southern Chinese garden feature to the context of Northern China. The process through which we approached the project reminded me of van Schaik's remark concerning tradition and innovation in our dialogue:

> I cannot think of these matters without reference to that reading that Mok Wei Wei has charged me with, especially the account of the process of poetry in *The Story of the Stone* in which the young protagonists compete to make a new poem, analysing each attempt for its awareness of pre-existing poems and for the wit with which a new nuance is added to what lies before. This seems to me an immaculate account of how creativity works.

Designing Amidst a Cultural Transformation

While I have described at length the origins of my "Chinese-ness" and the subsequent ways (mostly subconscious) in which it has informed my design approach, such mere attachment to one's ethnic culture is inadequate in Singapore if there is no engagement with its other cultures. With its history as a port-city and migrant society, Singapore has long had cross-cultural examples in its built environment – one of which is the ubiquitous shophouses in the city's historic quarters. They fused the Southern Chinese terrace-house typology with facades that incorporated an eclectic hybrid of Chinese, Malay and European classical elements.

From its inception, the practice has always maintained a strong interest in urban heritage and conservation issues, and has also renovated many shophouses. These range from the earliest example, Goh's House (1982–84), which reflected the heavy Peranakan taste of Dr Goh Poh Seng, FIG. 17 to later works such as Ristorante Da Paolo e Judie (1999–2001), which employed a sleek modernist language to interact with the traditional elements of the shophouse.[5] FIG. 18 In the early 2000s, we also got involved in the makeover of Singapore's civic and cultural district as the nation sought to develop itself into a global city for the arts. A series of municipal and educational buildings in the city centre were turned into cultural institutions.[6] FIG. 19 Besides their physical impact, these cultural institutions also began developing content that better defined the nation's sense of self and its relation to the world. For instance, the Asian Civilisations Museum's original mandate was to deepen the appreciation of the "great traditions" that Singapore's migrant society could be traced back to, showcasing Chinese, Indian and Islamic cultures, as well as its original collection of artefacts from indigenous Southeast Asia. This has since shifted towards narrating the histories of port-cities along the Maritime Silk Route and showcasing objects with cross-cultural influences. It is a change that emphasizes Singapore's historical role at the crossroads of trading, and the fact that we have always been shaped by globalization and multiculturalism.

Besides this cultural awakening, the early 2000s also saw Singapore open up public-sector projects to private firms, which allowed us to participate in projects such the National Museum of Singapore (2002–6) FIG. 20 and Victoria Theatre and Victoria Concert Hall (2009–14). FIG. 21 Both buildings were legacies of the colonial era situated in prime locations that required urban-design responses. Unlike earlier transformations, both of these projects retained their original functions. The National Museum of Singapore was originally the Raffles Library and Museum, while Victoria Theatre and Victoria Concert Hall, although originally built as the Town Hall and the Memorial Hall, had previously undergone changes of use in the early 1900s and 1980s respectively.

At the National Museum of Singapore, we conceptualized an "urban corridor" to link its original entrance facing the urban Bras Basah Park with a new entrance at the rear extension, which overlooks the historic Fort Canning Park. Emphasizing the contrast between the new and the old, the urban corridor features a series of spaces that allows visitors to experience the etchings of time as they travel along the public thoroughfare from the museum's historic Neo-Palladian architecture to its new, light and transparent extension, or vice versa. FIG. 22 In Victoria Theatre and Victoria Concert Hall, a historic passage between the two monuments, FIG. 23 which had over the years been relegated to a service corridor filled with equipment and ill-conceived structures, was restored to allow for free movement between the grand frontage of the complexes and the Old Parliament House situated behind. FIG. 24 Instead of making a strong contrast between the new interventions and the historic elements, a more nuanced approach was adopted to articulate the layering of histories. This ranged from the restoration of historic elements to the reinterpretation and reinstatement of lost details. FIG. 25 It also involved the recycling and repurposing of discarded elements from the recent past as well as the introduction of completely new ones. As a result, this monument is not only rejuvenated for contemporary use but also

FIG. 20 The extension of the National Museum of Singapore facing Fort Canning Park (2002–6).

FIG. 21 Victoria Theatre and Victoria Concert Hall (2009–14).

FIG. 22 In the National Museum of Singapore, the new annex's transparency contrasts with the solidity of the historic facade.

FIG. 23 The original passageway between Victoria Theatre and the then Memorial Hall.

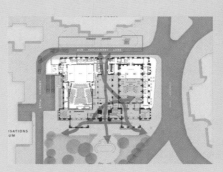

FIG. 24 Opening up the ground-floor spaces encouraged unimpeded movement between the two parts of Victoria Theatre and Victoria Concert Hall.

FIG. 25 A nuanced contrast is adopted between the reconstructed facade and the original one in Victoria Theatre and Victoria Concert Hall.

5 This outlet of the Da Paolo restaurant chain was closed in 2014.

6 The transformation started in 1989 when the former Empress Place Building, which housed various government offices, was converted to become the Empress Place Museum. This was followed in 1994 by the conversion of the old Tao Nan School to house the original, smaller Asian Civilisations Museum (ACM). In 2003, the Empress Place Building was renovated a second time when ACM took over the premises. Tao Nan School then became a dedicated museum to showcase Peranakan culture. In 1996, the former St Joseph's Institution on Bras Basah Road was refurbished to become the Singapore Art Museum, and this expanded in 2008 to include the former Catholic High School across the street. In 2004, the former Parliament House was converted into The Arts House, a multidisciplinary arts centre. The most recent transformation took place in 2015 when the former City Hall and Supreme Court were refurbished and integrated to become the National Gallery Singapore. Collectively, these changes have turned this district, located south from the mouth of the Singapore River, from a colonialist seat of power into the city-state's arts and culture precinct.

FIG. 26 Display of taxidermy specimens in the original Raffles Museum, now known as the National Museum of Singapore, c. 1931.

FIG. 27 The historic specimens exhibited in their new home at the Lee Kong Chian Natural History Museum (2011–15).

FIG. 28 The Lee Kong Chian Natural History Museum is a distinctive landmark in the campus of the National University of Singapore.

7 Van Schaik has written about this previously in various essays, including "Province and Metropolis/Funda Centre/ Belvedere Flats", *AA Files*, no. 14, 1987; "Province and Metropolis II", in *The Idea of the City*, ed. Robin Middleton (London: Architectural Association, 1996); and "Architecture in Asia: Province and Metropolis", in *Asian Architects Vol. 1*, ed. Tan Kok Meng (Singapore: Select Publishing, 2000).

8 A line by the French philosopher Jean Wahl, who van Schaik refers to earlier in the conversation.

retains the memories of the community that grew up using it.

Our relationship with the National Museum of Singapore, a building that was initially built in the nineteenth century to house a vast collection of tropical specimens, FIG. 26 came full circle when we won a competition to build the Lee Kong Chian Natural History Museum (2011–15) at the National University of Singapore. Besides creating an awareness of the importance of biodiversity and its conservation, this new museum was to house the original Raffles Collection of tropical specimens, FIG. 27 which had been displaced and left homeless for many years when the National Museum adopted its curatorial policy of showing artefacts instead of natural-history specimens. The new Natural History Museum is clustered around a plaza with the existing University Cultural Centre and the Yong Siew Toh Conservatory of Music, coming together to form a new focal point that celebrates the interaction of science, art and music. The museum's distinctive image of a "moss-covered rock" is a rare example of an iconic structure designed by the firm, which tends to veer towards space-making instead of form-making. FIG. 28

At the end of our dialogue in *Chinese More or Less*, van Schaik remarked that it is the interactions between spatial histories and contemporary concerns that generate what he termed as a "Provincial" actuality.[7] It is only by accounting for one's history in space and seeing how it functions as a creative input that "the spatiality of the architectural reality becomes overwhelmingly evident". He concluded by saying that "[a]s with poetry – 'the frothing of the hedges'[8] – revealing your lived drawings induces in others an awakening to their own deep spatial history. Singaporean spatial history is not peripheral, its difference to other spatial history is central to us all."

This has been the impetus for this monograph.

ONE OF THE PITFALLS OF TRYING TO TURN A TRADITION INTO A CONTEMPORARY ARCHITECTURAL EXPRESSION IS ENDING UP WITH A MERE LITERAL REPRESENTATION … IT IS NOT ABOUT MAKING DIRECT REFERENCES BY INCORPORATING SYMBOLS OF THE TRADITION, BUT SYNTHESIZING IT WITH NEW CONTEXTS AND WITH DIFFERENT IMPETUSES.

MORLEY ROAD HOUSE

1996 – 1999

The majority population in Singapore may be classified as Chinese, but that does not mean that all of them are attuned to the histories and cultures of China. It was thus rare to receive this commission for a house that references traditional Chinese architecture yet is suitable for modern living. Our design envisioned the house as a series of structures that frame movement and views to invoke the experience of a classical Chinese garden. In the same way as these gardens carefully choreograph a procession, the spaces in this two-storey house are crafted to create a path of delay and discovery that reveals four different sceneries.

Visitors enter the home through a courtyard that leads into a long, narrow gallery with a single framed view at the end. Walking towards it, they first arrive at a double-volume living room on the right. This "virtual pavilion" is furnished with classical Chinese furniture and is accompanied by a bamboo garden, offering a calm and tranquil welcome. Further down the path is another pavilion-like space. This dining area is flanked by water and a small fountain. There is also a framed view that hints at a third scenery hidden within the house. All is revealed when one leaves to stroll across a connecting bridge. As the overlapping walls and a willow tree give way to an enclosed garden foregrounded by a pool, visitors enter a two-storey pavilion that houses the

entertainment area. The journey is complete when visitors enter this garden and turn around to see a panoramic view of the house reflected by the pool.

While this sequence explores the principles of the Chinese garden, the concept of fragmenting the house was developed from our previous work with tropical bungalows. The result is a porous play between indoor and outdoor spaces. In spite of the house's classical traditions, its architectural language is uncompromisingly modern: white planar surfaces are juxtaposed against grey granite walls and aluminium-framed fenestration, while the entire residence is covered over with flat concrete roofs.

Morley Road House offers a conversation about abstraction and cultural reference. From the spirit of the classical Chinese garden emerges an architecture that is sensitive to the tropical climate and modern in outlook.

02

01 OPPOSITE The living room is visually extended to the exterior wall, which is adorned with a horizontal stone carving.

02 Main entrance.

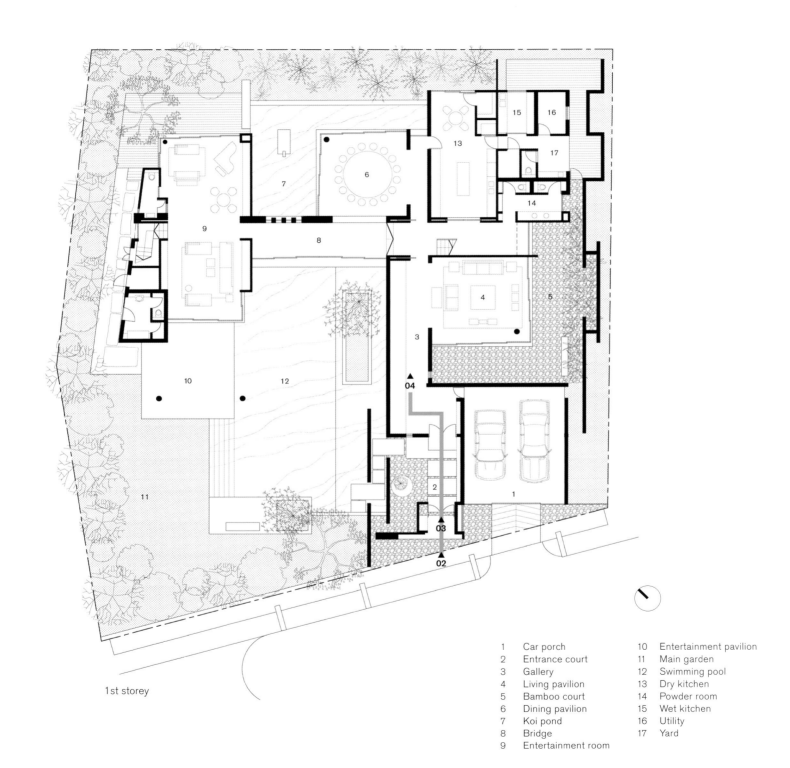

1st storey

1	Car porch	10	Entertainment pavilion
2	Entrance court	11	Main garden
3	Gallery	12	Swimming pool
4	Living pavilion	13	Dry kitchen
5	Bamboo court	14	Powder room
6	Dining pavilion	15	Wet kitchen
7	Koi pond	16	Utility
8	Bridge	17	Yard
9	Entertainment room		

03

04

03 Entrance court.

04 View along gallery from foyer.

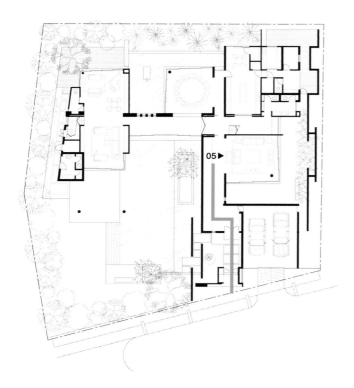

05

05 Living pavilion opening out to the bamboo courtyard.

06 Dining pavilion opening out to the surrounding koi pond.

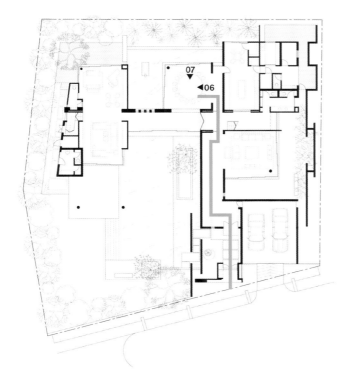

07

07 A glimpse of the main garden from the dining room.

08

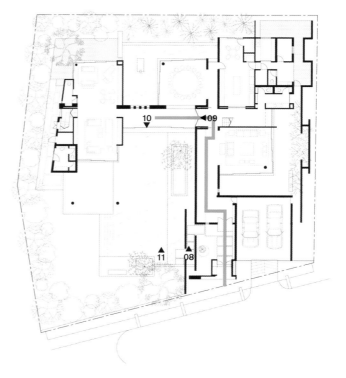

08 Overlapping garden walls conceal views of the main garden.

09

10

09 Crossing the bridge …

10 … to reveal the view of the swimming pool and garden beyond.

11 OVERLEAF Looking back at the house from the main garden.

RISTORANTE DA PAOLO E JUDIE

1999–2001

The shophouse typology in Singapore is a product of different cultures coming together. Its long and narrow plan, with walls on both sides supporting timber joists, has its origins in Southern China. However, its facade – a hybrid of elements including Corinthian motifs, French windows and Malay fretwork fascia boards – reflects adaptations made within the Southeast-Asian context. It is in one such shophouse that we designed a restaurant for Italian eatery Da Paolo e Judie.

We first identified features worth retaining in this three-storey conserved shophouse located in Chinatown. As its facade and light well proved to be authentic, a sequence of spaces was then woven through them to orchestrate a dialogue between the existing architecture and our interventions.

Guests enter through the restaurant's high-walled forecourt and are welcomed by a 3-by-3-metre (10-by-10-foot) pivoting timber door that opens into an enigmatic "tunnel". This passageway-cum-lounge is clad in dark-stained teak panels, with concealed lighting in vertical recesses. At the end of this tunnel, a burst of light from the shophouse's triple-volume light well floods an entirely white space. This reception area is furnished with a bar counter and staircase that are both finished with polished reconstituted marble and stainless steel.

The elegant entrance is a subtle prelude. The dining hall above has walls of maple-veneered panels, which are sensuously wrapped in glass and illuminated above and below by concealed lighting. This "light box" is punctuated by the shophouse's existing features – including its front and rear facade shutters, as well as the light well – to create a sophisticated backdrop of light, shade and reflection that elevates the dining experience.

The modernity of this interior is juxtaposed against the traditional shophouse space. By lining up the services along one side of the party wall, diners can experience the full width of the shophouse's narrow facades and the continuous flow of space from front to back. Just as the shophouse is a home to contrasting cultures, this restaurant interior offers an experience through darkness and light, as well as through old and new.

01

01 The shophouse facade is a reflection of hybrid cultures.

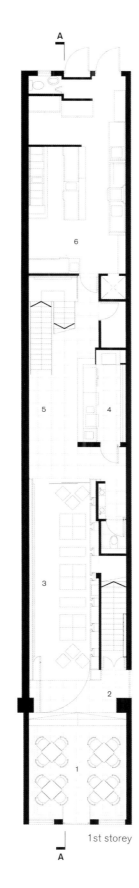

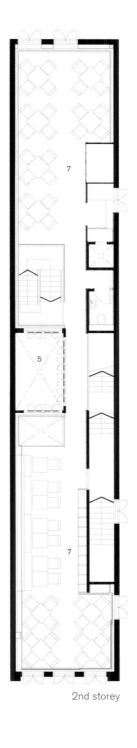

1st storey

2nd storey

3rd storey

1   Forecourt
2   Main entrance
3   Lounge
4   Bar
5   Light well
6   Kitchen
7   Dining
8   Private dining

1	Forecourt	5	Kitchen
2	Main entrance	6	Dining
3	Lounge	7	Private dining
4	Light well		

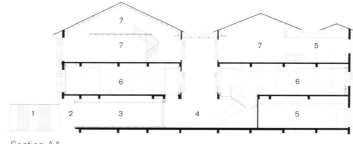

Section AA

02

03

02 The lounge articulated as a darkened passage.

03 Looking back to the high-walled forecourt from the lounge.

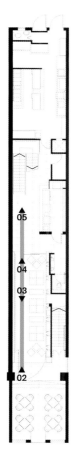

04

05

04 Approaching the light well.

05 A sleek staircase in the light well leading to the second-storey dining area.

06

07

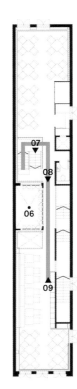

06 Timber shutters arrayed on the facade of the
triple-volume light well.

07 Arriving at the reception of the dining area.

08

08 The dining area is sensuously wrapped in a glass skin that is punctuated by openings to the light well or the exterior.

09 OVERLEAF The journey through the shophouse plays on lightness and darkness as it does upon the old and the new.

SPOTTISWOODE PARK HOUSE

1999–2002

This shophouse is sited on a plot with highly unusual proportions. Its front is only 3 metres (10 feet) wide and this tapers to 2.4 metres (7 ⁵⁄₆ feet) at the rear. Between them is an extremely elongated space that measures 33 metres (108 feet) in length.

We divided the site into two living zones. At the front is the conserved main building, which has its own air well over a koi pond. This was designated for the owner, a Shakespearean scholar who lectures at a university. At the back of this house, we built a new annex for her elderly mother. These two homes meet at an open-to-sky courtyard, which allows for activities to overlap while keeping the living quarters separate.

On the first storey, the courtyard is largely enjoyed by the annex – it is accessible to the main building only from a sunken dining area, from where a low, horizontal window frames a view of the courtyard's light-filled space. The two homes connect in various ways on the second storey above the courtyard. A small terrace on one side of the party wall links the main building's second-storey living room to a small

guestroom within the annex. Across this wall, an ascending flight of steps links to a roof garden that sits above the bedroom of the annex. This allows the owner to enjoy the entire length of the site without infringing on the privacy of her mother.

These various connections result in a shophouse that offers multiple intimate spaces strung along its lengthy envelope. Each enjoys its own views and offers a different quality of light. In contrast to these intimate nooks running horizontally through the house, its spaces gradually open up as one moves from the ground floor up to the roof terrace.

02

01 OPPOSITE The shophouse, sandwiched between two larger neighbours. All photographs were taken in 2019.
02 Entrance to the house from the five-foot way.

9

14

10a

10b

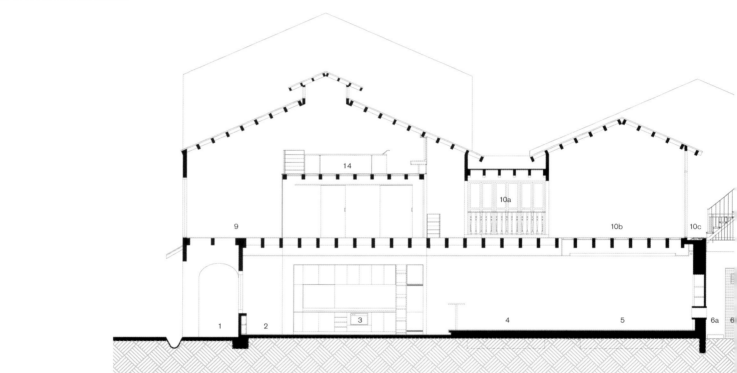

Section AA

1

2

3

4

5

10c

15a

15b

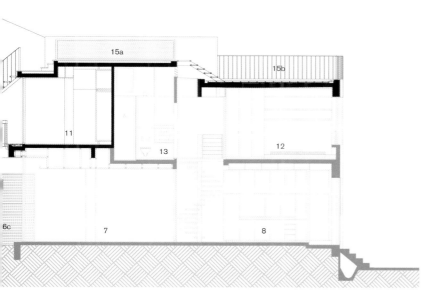

1	Five-foot way	9	Master bedroom
2	Foyer	10	Living and terrace
3	Kitchen	11	Guest room
4	Decorative pond	12	Master bedroom (annex)
5	Sunken dining	13	Bathroom
6	Courtyard	14	Attic study
7	Living (annex)	15	Roof terrace
8	Kitchen/dining (annex)		

6b

6a

6c

7

8

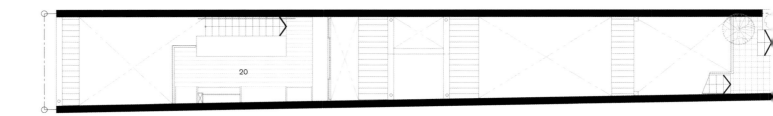

Attic

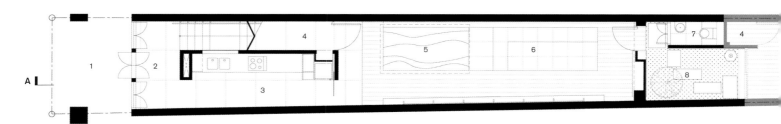

2nd storey

A

1st storey

1	Five-foot way	12	Master bathroom
2	Foyer	13	Wardrobe
3	Kitchen	14	Corridor
4	Store	15	Living
5	Decorative pond	16	Terrace
6	Sunken dining	17	Guest room
7	Powder room	18	Master bedroom (annex)
8	Courtyard	19	Bathroom
9	Living (annex)	20	Attic study
10	Kitchen/dining (annex)	21	Roof terrace
11	Master bedroom		

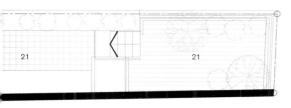

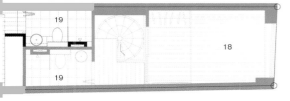

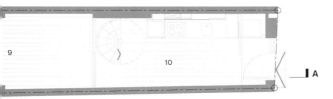

03

04

03 The light well in the conserved house viewed from second storey.

04 Uninterrupted view from the attic to the first-storey space.

05 OVERLEAF View of the light well and pond from a hobby table in the sunken dining area. The house is filled with the owner's books and artefacts.

06

06 Looking up from the courtyard between the conserved house and the new annex.

07 Looking down from the roof terrace to the living room.

08 The roofscape of the conserved shophouse against the backdrop of a public-housing development, a contrast of old and new.

07

08

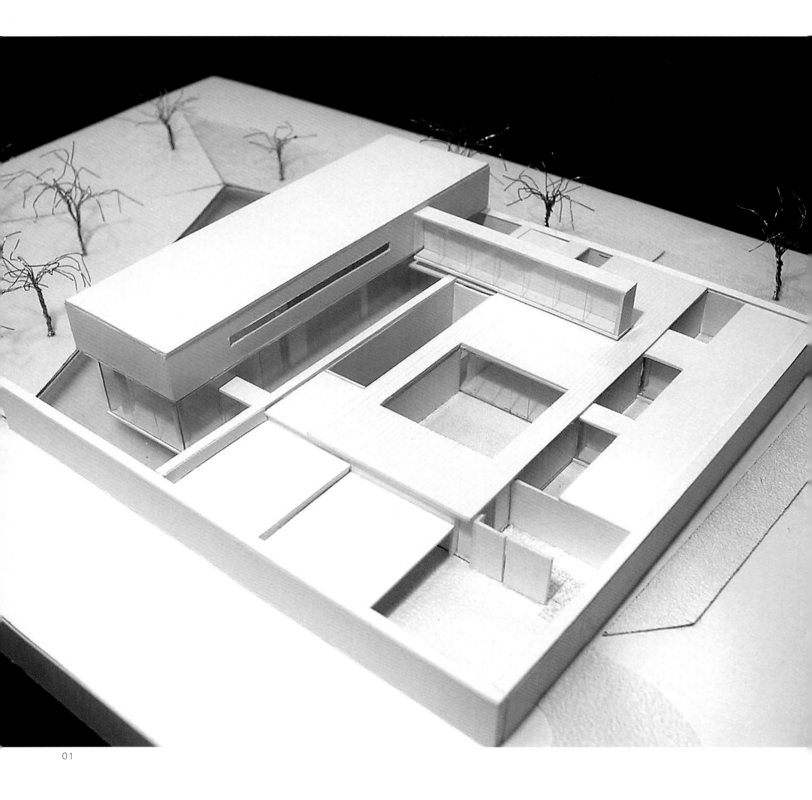

01

01 One half of the house is an enclosed
environment punctuated by courtyards.

BEIJING HOUSE

2004

Chinese architect Chang Yung Ho (张永和) invited us to design a house as part of a showcase of works by architects of Chinese descent based both in China and overseas. Each architect was assigned a plot of 1,266 square metres (13,600 square feet) that contained a "spatial riddle" expressed in different configurations of a series of 4-metre (13-foot) walls. In the plan view, these walled plots recalled ancient Chinese characters, offering a unifying theme for this development on the outskirts of Beijing.

Our plot had a wall that divided the site. One half was entirely enclosed, while the other opened up to a canal. This was our starting point in designing this proposal for a house that explored spaces of dualities – a play of inward and outward views, and also of compressed and released sequences.

On the fully enclosed side, we inserted a one-storey floor plate that is punctuated with courtyards. In this chessboard-like arrangement, each residential quarter sits amidst a private courtyard that offers intimate worlds for enjoying solitude and serenity. This is in contrast to the open garden across the wall. A single free-standing structure seemingly

floats above a moat of water. Looking out into the garden, this two-storey grand pavilion houses the formal living and dining areas on the ground floor and the master suite above.

In a homage to traditional Chinese spaces, we also crafted a highly choreographed journey for the house guests. Approaching from the road, the flat wall of the house conceals its interiors, just like the hutongs of Beijing. Upon entry, the guests make their way through carefully screened views of the private dwellings, an experience akin to walking through a Chinese garden. They finally arrive at the grand pavilion, and are rewarded with an expansive view of the canal and beyond.

02

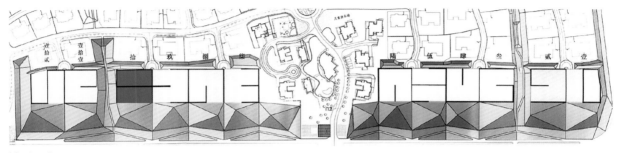

Master plan

02 The other half of the house is expressed as a free-standing pavilion in the garden.

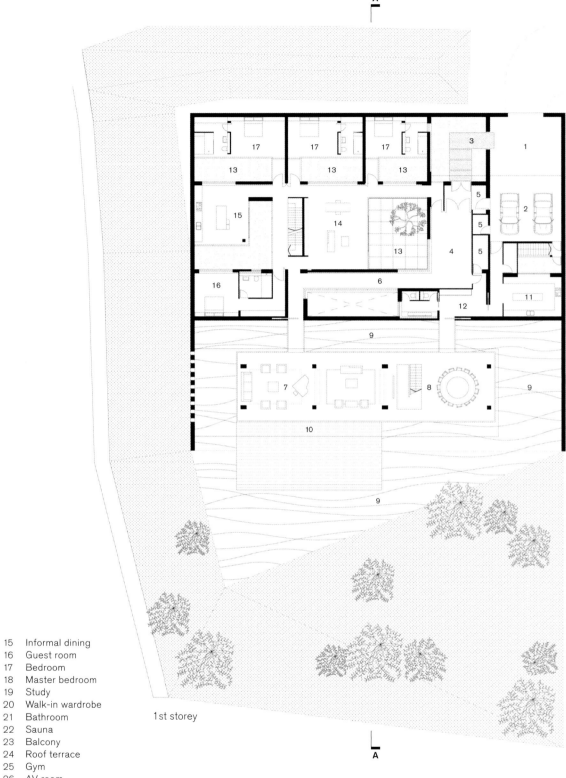

1st storey

1   Driveway
2   Car porch
3   Entrance court
4   Foyer
5   Stores
6   Gallery
7   Formal living
8   Formal dining
9   Reflecting pool
10 Terrace
11 Kitchen
12 Servery
13 Courtyard
14 Library/family area
15 Informal dining
16 Guest room
17 Bedroom
18 Master bedroom
19 Study
20 Walk-in wardrobe
21 Bathroom
22 Sauna
23 Balcony
24 Roof terrace
25 Gym
26 AV room
27 Sunken courtyard

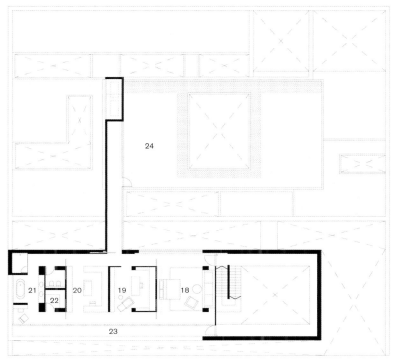

2nd storey

03

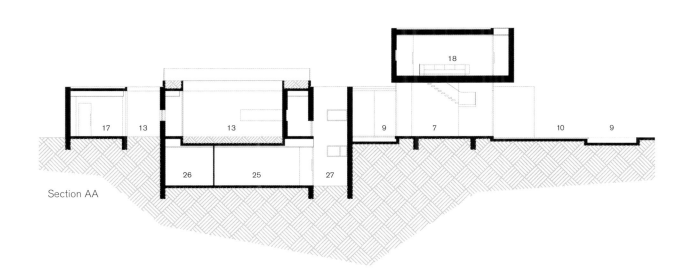

Section AA

03 Car porch.

04

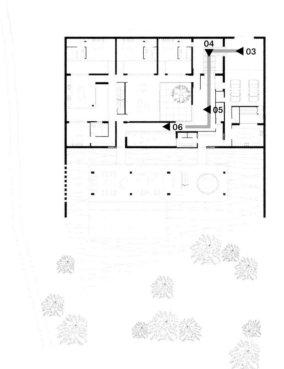

04 Entrance court.

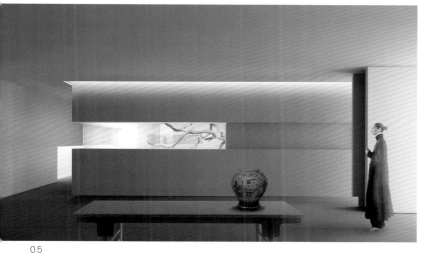

05

06

05 From the entrance foyer, a glimpse of the courtyard in the private quarters.

06 Along the gallery, a view of the sunken courtyard.

07

07 Crossing the threshold into the transparent pavilion,
with an expansive view of the garden beyond.

08

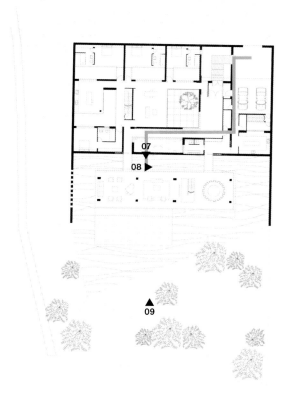

07

08

▲
09

08 A reflecting pool surrounds the pavilion.

09 OVERLEAF The double-storey pavilion floats above the reflecting pool.

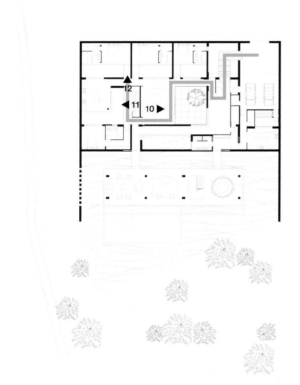

10

10 Within the private quarter, an intimate courtyard adjoining
the library and informal sitting room evokes a sense of solitude.

11

12

11 The informal dining room is bounded by a courtyard.

12 A walled courtyard dwells within each bedroom, creating a series of little secluded worlds.

01

NATIONAL MUSEUM OF SINGAPORE

2002–2006

First developed as the Raffles Library and Museum by the British in 1887, this institution at the foot of Fort Canning Hill has been expanded several times in parallel with Singapore's historical development. In 2002, the national monument underwent a four-year-long refurbishment, including the addition of a new wing, as part of efforts to transform Singapore into a cultural destination.

We were brought on to the project when construction was about to start on an original scheme by CPG Consultants. This meant working within constraints, including the decision to house most of the programme underground, as well as retaining such key elements as the physical marker at the corner of the new wing. As the museum sits between two major historical green spaces – Bras Basah Park and Fort Canning Hill – we envisioned it as an urban corridor between them. This meant creating an architectural expression that would connect the two, as well as connecting the new with the old. Our approach was less about formal intervention than the creation of a series of spaces that would let visitors experience the movement of time as they walked between the museum's Neo-Palladian architecture and its new glass-and-aluminium extension.

03

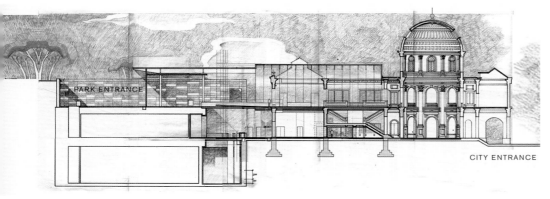

PARK ENTRANCE

CITY ENTRANCE

02

01 A glass connector cuts through the original tiled roof, from which a whale's skeleton had once been suspended. This intervention allows the dome over the entrance rotunda to be viewed up close.

02 Urban corridor study sketch by Nui Ratiwat.

03 The whale skeleton *in situ*, c. 1910.

The Old Museum

Entering from Bras Basah, visitors are greeted by the original building's iconic rotunda and a grand staircase. This leads them to the second-floor galleries, where they encounter a glass connector that cuts through the original tiled roof to reveal part of the museum's historic structure. This feature brings the museum's dome closer to visitors, and the view is enhanced at night by the beautiful lighting and by reflections on the glass. It also physically links the old building with the new extension further in. Standing underneath the connector, visitors look into the original building where there are two thematic galleries. Turning around, they see the rear wings added in 1907 and, further on, a transparent glass atrium that opens up to the hills of Fort Canning.

On the museum's historic facade, we included certain unexpected touches to signal the introduction of new elements. For instance, the timber shutters of the newly conserved building were painted metallic silver, a contemporary colour not typically used on traditional elements. However, this elegantly echoes the museum's iconic dome, which is covered with zinc fish-scale tiles. This approach of respecting the old while not embracing it entirely was also used on the rotunda, as we painted its ornaments in white instead of using colour to highlight them. They stand out against the rotunda's inner walls, which are in a darker shade of white, subtly accentuating the spatial depth.

04

05

04 The original rotunda, *c.* 1931.   **05** The main facade facing the city entrance.

06

06 The refurbished rotunda.

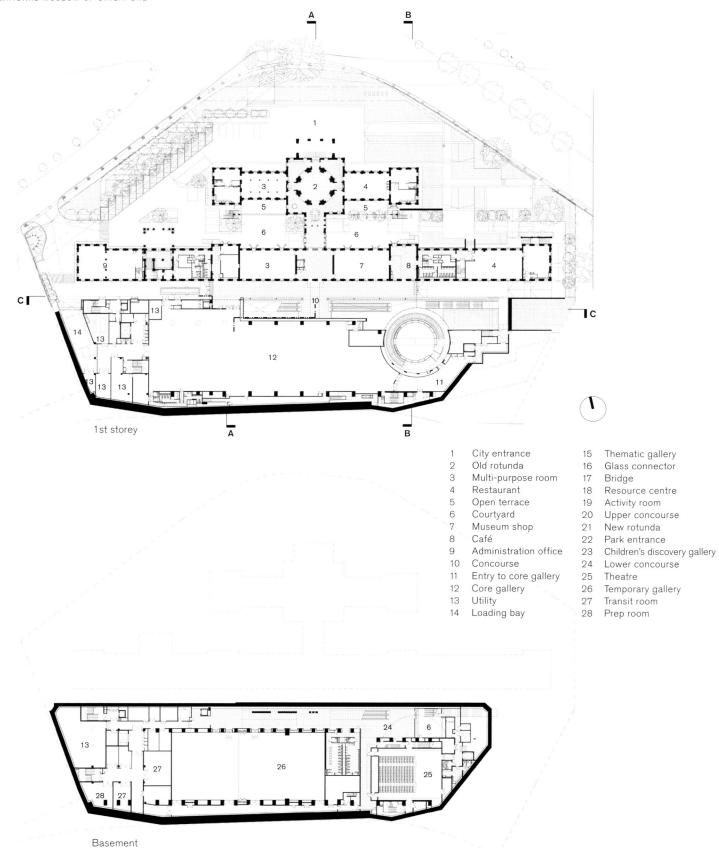

1st storey

Basement

1	City entrance	15	Thematic gallery
2	Old rotunda	16	Glass connector
3	Multi-purpose room	17	Bridge
4	Restaurant	18	Resource centre
5	Open terrace	19	Activity room
6	Courtyard	20	Upper concourse
7	Museum shop	21	New rotunda
8	Café	22	Park entrance
9	Administration office	23	Children's discovery gallery
10	Concourse	24	Lower concourse
11	Entry to core gallery	25	Theatre
12	Core gallery	26	Temporary gallery
13	Utility	27	Transit room
14	Loading bay	28	Prep room

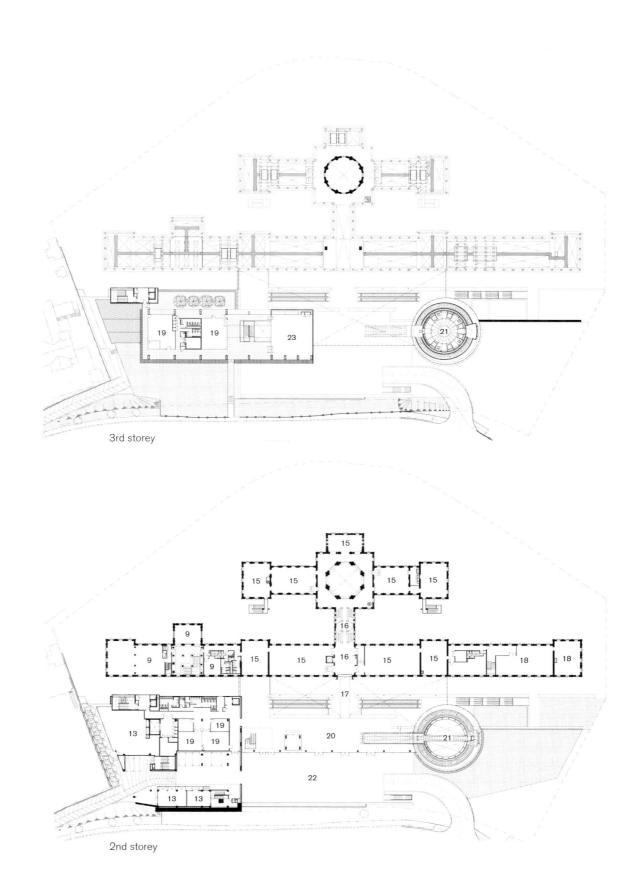

3rd storey

2nd storey

The New Annex

A markedly different experience awaits visitors arriving at the museum from Fort Canning. Amidst the lush setting of nature, a rectilinear volume sheathed in champagne gold announces the museum's name like a billboard. Visitors arrive at an expansive entrance court that extends into the driveway, and are confronted by a retaining wall that seemingly cuts into Fort Canning. This wall is clad in horizontal bands of pre-cast black-pigmented concrete up to four metres (13 feet) in length. Each "institutional-scale" band is executed in various textures by hand to express the stratification of geological layers within the landscape. As the annex houses the subterranean galleries, the effect suggests an archaeological dig, in an area where ancient settlements going as far back as the fourteenth century have previously been unearthed.

Physically connecting the new annex and the old building is a bridge clad in stainless steel that heightens one's awareness of the transition from present to past. This was a response to a conservation law that dictated a 6-metre (20-foot) gap between the museum and the annex. The movement between the old museum's more cellular space to a total immersion within Fort Canning was realized with glass, a contemporary material that is often used to contrast with classical buildings.

The sublime use of materials and the considered connections come together to impart a sense of how the building has evolved over time. This also reflects the history of the museum: a palimpsest that allows visitors to move through layers of history, space and material.

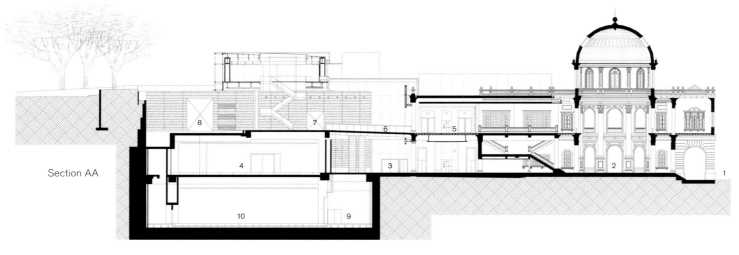

Section AA

1	City entrance	6	Bridge
2	Old rotunda	7	Upper concourse
3	Concourse	8	Park entrance
4	Core gallery	9	Lower concourse
5	Glass connector	10	Temporary gallery

07 A succession of spaces from new to old, suggesting the layering of history.

08 OVERLEAF The new, light-filled annex introduces views of Fort Canning Hill.

10

11

09 The structure of the new annex is set away from the historic facade.

10 A site-specific art installation in the form of a digital wall by artist Matthew Ngui.

11 The excavation carried out to build the new annex is recalled by the use of pre-cast panels to clad the basement walls – these are of varying textures and sizes, akin to the striations of rock.

12

13

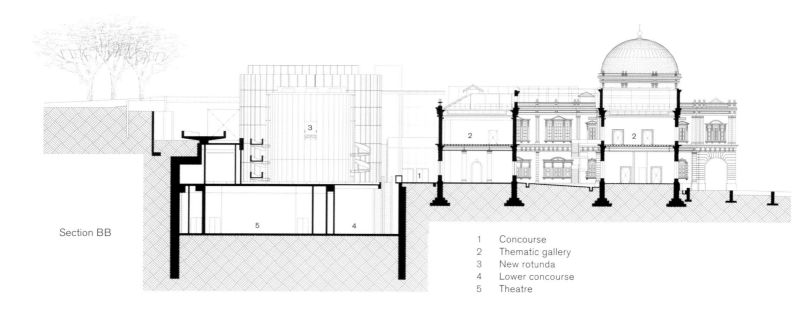

Section BB

1 Concourse
2 Thematic gallery
3 New rotunda
4 Lower concourse
5 Theatre

12 View of the upper and lower concourses from the children's gallery on the third level.

13 Looking across the upper concourse towards the new rotunda.

14 Within the new rotunda, a ramp leads to the core gallery on the lower level.

14

15

16

15 & 16 Flights of escalators connect the lower concourse
to the basement.

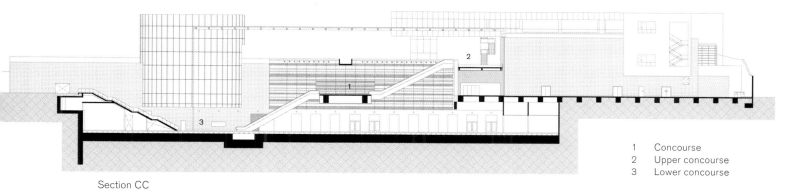

Section CC

1 Concourse
2 Upper concourse
3 Lower concourse

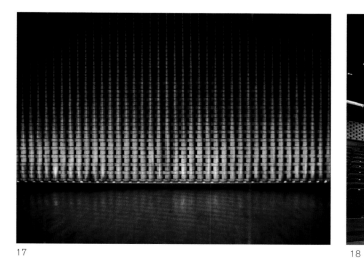

17

18

17 Detail of the brick lattice work.

18 Brick lattice walls within the black-box theatre.
19 OVERLEAF Facade of the new annex facing Fort Canning Hill.

VICTORIA THEATRE
AND VICTORIA CONCERT HALL

2009 – 2014

We were not the first to renovate these national monuments, both over a century old. Victoria Theatre was originally built as Singapore's Town Hall in 1862. Just over four decades later, it was joined by both the Victoria Memorial Hall and the clock tower that connects the two buildings, while in 1909 it was converted into Victoria Theatre. During the mid-twentieth century, both the theatre and the hall underwent renovations. While the former was expanded in the 1950s to increase its seating capacity, the latter was converted in the late 1970s to house the newly formed Singapore Symphony Orchestra, at which point it was renamed the Victoria Concert Hall.

When we embarked on this project in 2009, we were confronted by a series of unsympathetic renovations undertaken during the twentieth century that had severely altered the integrity of these historic structures. The theatre had lost a facade, destroying the courtyard it shared with the concert hall. Its original double-volume lobby on the ground floor was also squashed by a new mezzanine level. The concert hall was in better condition, but several new columns, created to support a large balcony, now landed rather intrusively in the ground-floor lobby.

We still recall how the client summarized the brief: "Restore the monument to its former glory and give us state-of-the-art performing venues." Working within the constraints of the historic envelope to create a modern space, our approach was to optimize rather than maximize the buildings. Architecturally, we wanted to retain, reinstate and renew built elements from the different periods. Each of these distinctive forms was to be held together by a twenty-first-century refurbishment, layer by layer. It is not unlike a piece of Baroque music, in which different parts – soprano, alto, tenor, bass – all have their own distinctive melodies but, when woven together, interact with each other to form one cohesive composition. The aim was to create a dialogue between the buildings' original Neoclassical elements and our contemporary interventions.

01

01 The demolition of the original Edwardian theatre in 1954.
02 Victoria Theatre and Victoria Concert Hall in Empress Place.

03 The refurbished facades of Victoria Theatre and Victoria Concert Hall.

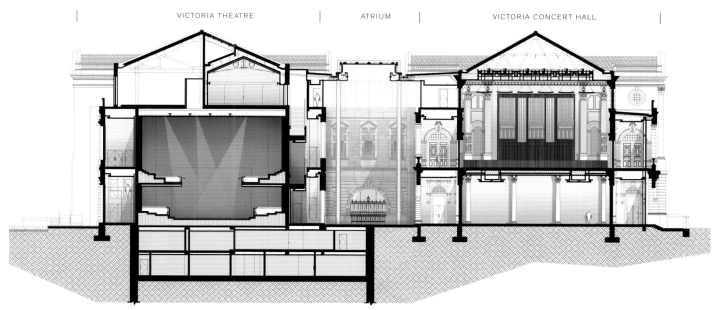

VICTORIA THEATRE   ATRIUM   VICTORIA CONCERT HALL

Cross-section AA of the design proposal

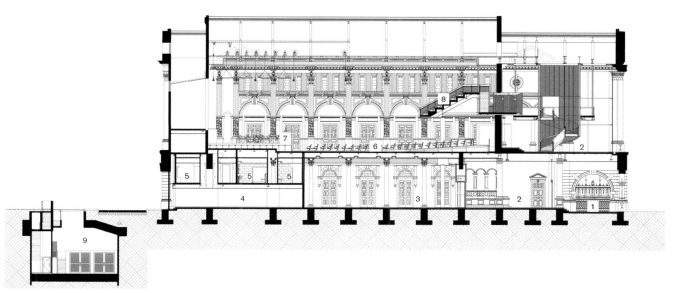

Section BB

1   Concert-hall porch
2   Concert-hall foyer
3   Ancillary space
4   Concert-hall office
5   Orchestra toilet/
    changing room
6   Concert hall
7   Orchestra platform
8   Concert-hall balcony seats
9   M&E spaces

The Atrium

The courtyard between the two buildings is the focal point of this reconciliation. Facing the clock tower, the historic facade of the concert hall is on the left; across from it, we have reinstated the lost theatre facade based on archival drawings. Instead of an exact Neoclassical replica, this new wall is clad in pre-cast concrete panels and the motifs have been flattened to appear as incisions on the surface. This contemporary interpretation of the past is a subtle contrast to the pronounced plasterwork found on the concert hall opposite.

This juxtaposition was enhanced by the decision to roof over the courtyard to create an atrium and grand lobby for both performing venues. Not only does this reinstate a historic passageway, it also ensures that the buildings are open and porous again. Various services that had been built in the courtyard over the years were relocated. The public can now walk from the buildings' front plaza through to Parliament Lane at the back, connecting the institution to the Empress Place precinct, where many of Singapore's historic buildings still stand.

06

04   05

04 The original open-air passageway between the Memorial Hall (now Victoria Concert Hall) and the theatre.

05 The passageway was blocked and cluttered with services in the years before the refurbishment, as in this photograph of *c.* 2009.

06 Entrance ramp leading to the central atrium.

07 OPPOSITE Central atrium with a view of the clock tower. To the left is the restored facade of Victoria Concert Hall; to the right, the reconstructed facade of Victoria Theatre.

08

08 The reconstructed facade of Victoria Theatre, clad in pre-cast panels.

09

09 The restored facade of Victoria Concert Hall.   **10 OVERLEAF** View of the atrium from second-level terrace.

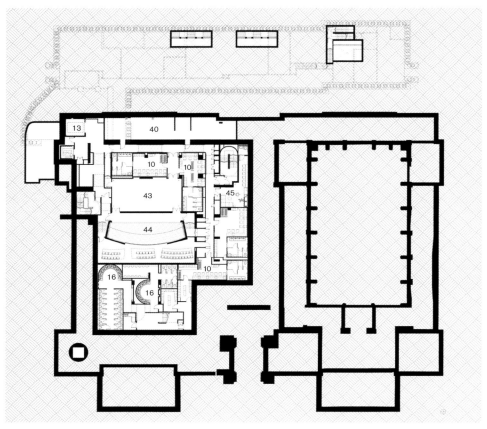

Basement 1

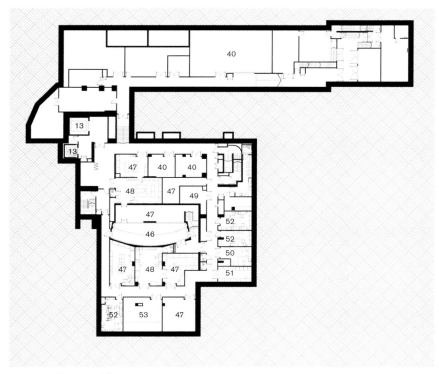

Basement 2

1   Central atrium
2   Arcade
3   Lift lobby
4   Theatre porch
5   Theatre foyer
6   VIP lounge
7   Theatre stall seats
8   Stage
9   Wing
10 Theatre backstage
11 Theatre backstage entry
12 Loading/unloading
13 Service lift for theatre and concert hall
14 Concert-hall porch
15 Concert-hall foyer
16 Toilet
17 Bar
18 Ancillary space
19 Concert-hall office
20 Kitchen
21 Concert-hall backstage entry
22 Orchestra toilet/changing room
23 Back projector room
24 Control room
25 VIP box
26 Theatre circle seats
27 Central office

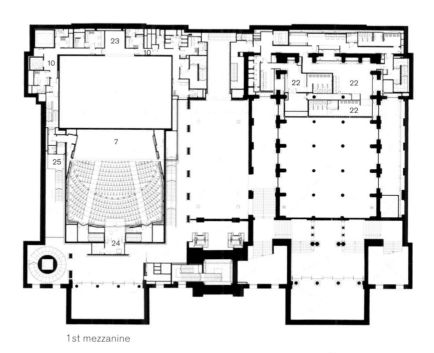

1st mezzanine

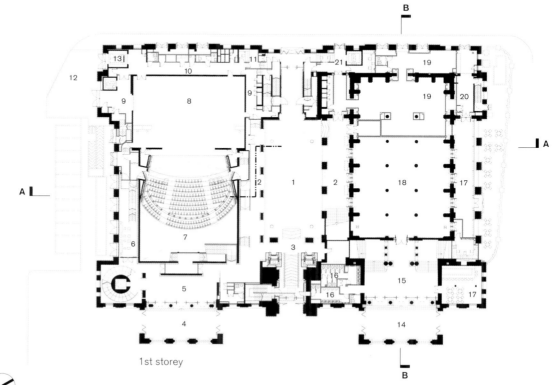

1st storey

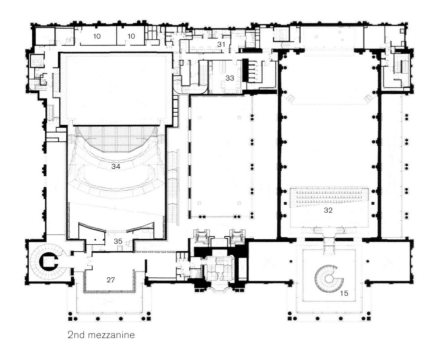

2nd mezzanine

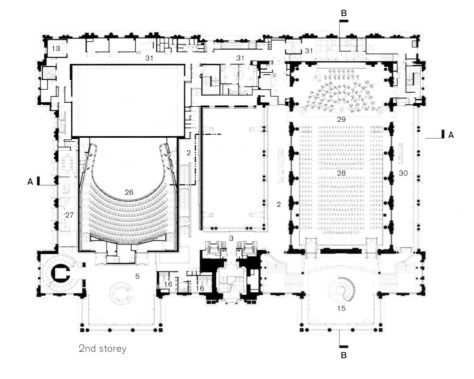

2nd storey

1   Central atrium
2   Arcade
3   Lift lobby
4   Theatre porch
5   Theatre foyer
6   VIP lounge
7   Theatre stall seats
8   Stage
9   Wing
10 Theatre backstage
11 Theatre backstage entry
12 Loading/unloading
13 Service lift for theatre and concert hall
14 Concert-hall porch
15 Concert-hall foyer
16 Toilet
17 Bar
18 Ancillary space
19 Concert-hall office
20 Kitchen
21 Concert-hall backstage entry
22 Orchestra toilet/changing room
23 Back projector room
24 Control room
25 VIP box
26 Theatre circle seats
27 Central office

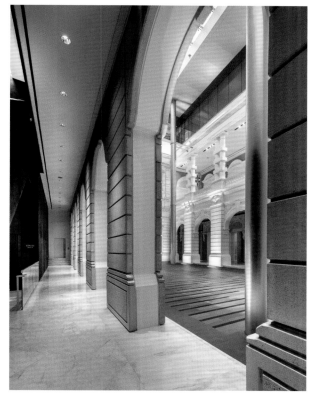

11 Refurbished arcade of Victoria Theatre.

12 Refurbished arcade of Victoria Concert Hall.

28 Concert hall
29 Orchestra platform
30 VIP lounge
31 Concert-hall backstage
32 Concert-hall balcony seats
33 Orchestra green room
34 Lighting bridge
35 Followspot room
36 Music rehearsal room
37 Dance/drama
   rehearsal room
38 Service deck
39 Hoist/control-gear room
40 M&E spaces
41 Audio-recording room
42 Outdoor terrace
43 Trap room
44 Orchestra pit
45 Theatre green room
46 Orchestra pit mechanism
47 Store
48 Workshop
49 Sound patch
50 Costumes
51 Laundry
52 Office
53 Music-archive library

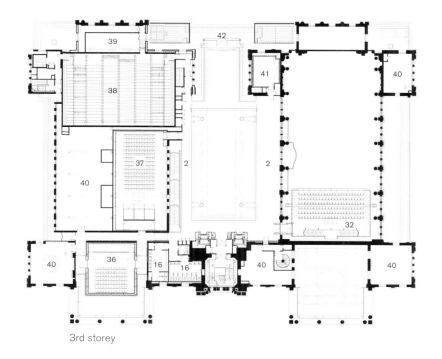

3rd storey

Victoria Theatre

By removing the 1950s renovation and inserting a completely new auditorium, we continued the conversation between past and present already underway in the atrium. As visitors move from the concert hall's original Neoclassical facade, past the theatre's new facade with its historical provenance, they then encounter the exterior of the theatre's auditorium. Flat and devoid of decoration, this is clad in large, black GRC (glassfibre reinforced concrete) panels, and it serves to bookend the transition from restoration to intervention.

When designing the interior of the theatre, we struggled with the options of either referencing its original Edwardian design or creating a completely new space. Neither seemed ideal. There were insufficient records available to achieve the former in a satisfactory manner, while pursuing the latter would not reflect the theatre's place in the community. While its 1950s interior was unremarkable, it contained about one thousand chairs highly evocative of their time. These British products were recycled for use in our modern but scaled-down 614-seat auditorium. The old chairs' small cast-iron and aluminium connectors – one kidney-shaped, the other U-shaped – were employed as datum lines on the auditorium walls. Solid timbers were extruded that followed the profiles of these recycled components, and then fixed to them to form a screen that performed acoustic functions. The chairs' backrests were utilized as cladding for a new structure suspended in the second-storey foyer that houses the music rehearsal rooms. This floating Rubik's Cube of chairs, with original seat numbers intact and timber surfaces unrestored, will hopefully bring back memories for a generation that grew up using the theatre.

14

13 OPPOSITE The layering of the construction: the historic facade of Victoria Concert Hall (right); the reinterpreted pre-cast-panelled wall of Victoria Theatre (centre); and the new GRC-panel wall of the theatre auditorium (left).

14 The new spiral staircase in the theatre.

15

16

17

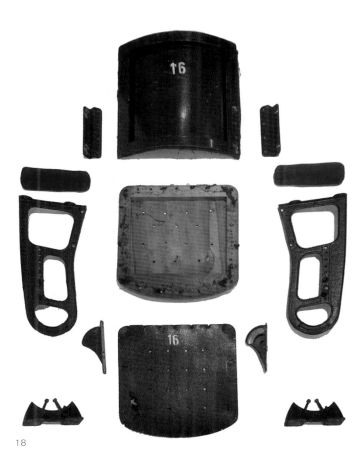

18

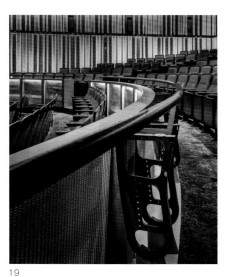

19

20

15 & 16 OPPOSITE The unrestored backrests of the original 1950s theatre chairs have been re-employed as panelling in the foyer.

17 The chairs were manufactured in Britain in the 1950s.

18 The component parts of the original theatre chairs.

19 The cast-iron legs have been recycled as railing stanchions.

20 The connectors between the chairs now line the walls to support the timber lattice work.

21 OVERLEAF The intimately scaled Victoria Theatre viewed from the stage.

Victoria Concert Hall

As the concert hall was in relatively good condition, and was for the most part historically intact, it was rehabilitated with minimal intervention. One of the key tasks was to restore the main lobby, which had acquired eight rather intrusive columns, including two that landed in the middle of its grand Neoclassical staircase. These were built during the renovation in the late 1970s, and supported a new balcony and mezzanine foyer in the concert hall's second storey.

The balcony was rebuilt to be smaller and higher. It is now suspended from five steel rods, with two columns at the front. The columns land in a multi-purpose space on the ground floor (now housing a restaurant) and are not visible in the foyer. The smaller balcony also improves both views and acoustics for audiences seated below. Overall, the 673-seater hall allows for more acoustic reverberation, producing a warmer tone for the concerts. This was achieved by replacing the existing vaulted ceiling with a coffered design that harmonizes with the proportions of the hall. In addition, bulky sound reflectors were replaced with lightweight acrylic panels that are aesthetically pleasing and make the space more open.

Out in the triple-volume foyer, the new mezzanine lobby does away with the need for columns completely. Instead, it is suspended by eight steel rods and is anchored by a spiral staircase in the middle. Enclosed in an intricate stainless-steel mesh, the staircase glows like a large light sculpture, drawing in audiences – even from the streets outside.

22 Plaster mouldings over the grand stairway of Victoria Concert Hall.

23

24

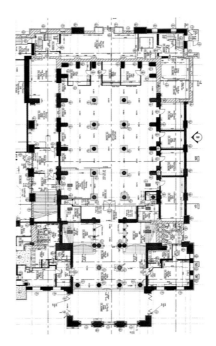

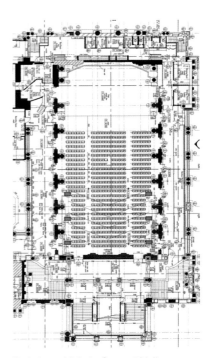

1st storey Victoria Concert Hall

2nd storey Victoria Concert Hall

25

23 Columns built to support the concert hall's balcony in the 1970s intruded into the foyer space – see plans to the right showing the columns in red before the renovation.

24 A pair of columns even appeared in the middle of the grand stairways.

25 The restored ancillary space on the first storey of Victoria Concert Hall.

26 The restored foyer of Victoria Concert Hall.

27 The restored grand stairway of Victoria Concert Hall.

26

27

29

30

28 OPPOSITE A new spiral staircase in
the concert hall's foyer brings audiences up
to the balcony level. The contemporary
chandelier was commissioned to complement
the restored interior.

29 Staircase leading to the balcony level.

30 View of the concert hall from the new balcony.

31 OVERLEAF View of the restored concert hall with the
new balcony.

32

33

The Clock Tower

Sitting atop the 54-metre (148-foot) tower is a clock and a set of bells installed in 1906. As part of the restoration, our conservation consultant tracked down the original British manufacturer, Gillett & Johnston of Croydon. Not only were they still in business, the company had even kept the original order that The Straits Trading Company Limited had made for the "Westminster" quarter chime clock. The clock's mechanism was dismantled for restoration in the United Kingdom, and it was repainted in the original gold and cobalt blue. The timber structures holding the mechanism in the tower were also stripped of later paint layers to showcase their natural state. As the clock bell was too heavy to move, its cracks were repaired *in situ*. The clock face was replaced with an acrylic version.

While the clock was previously operated manually, we requested that it be made semi-automatic so that an employee no longer needed to climb the tower every other day to wind and maintain it. In addition, a new staircase was installed in the tower to make it easier to access. This porous design turns the clock's counterweights, previously hidden to one side, into a feature by suspending them in an exposed cage in the middle. Today, the inside of the tower is accessible to the public on guided tours.

34

35

36

37

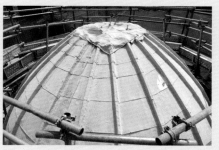

38

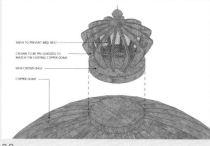

39

Late in the restoration work, we discovered that the tower's dome had once been topped by an ornament, which had since gone missing. Based on the few available historic photographs, it was concluded that this crown-like feature was probably built in commemoration of Queen Victoria, and had been removed in the 1950s when many colonial symbols were being discarded.

As the original ornament could not be tracked down, and no reliable drawings or photos exist, we designed a re-interpretation to act as the new lightning conductor, capturing the crown's original silhouette using simple modern lines. Together with the restoration of the clock, this contemporary cap on the building's copper dome was the final step in returning the tower to its former glory.

40

32 A 19th-century catalogue from Gillett & Johnston, Croydon.

33 The restored clock mechanism painted in period-appropriate gold and cobalt blue.

34 The clock face and the timber structure holding the mechanism.

35 & 36 A new staircase was installed in the tower to facilitate maintenance access.

37 An undated image showing the dome topped by an ornament, possibly a crown, which was probably removed in the 1950s.

38 During construction, it was discovered that the top of the dome had been dismantled.

39 A new ornament was designed to echo the silhouette of the missing original.

40 The hoisting of the new ornament at the end of the refurbishment works.

LEE KONG CHIAN
NATURAL HISTORY MUSEUM

2011–2015

Amidst a resurgence of interest in biodiversity and sustainability, this museum was conceived to give Singapore's significant Zoological Reference Collection a proper home once again. This set of natural-history specimens, formerly known as the Raffles Collection, dates back to the late nineteenth century when the Raffles Library and Museum began collecting examples from across Southeast Asia.

We won an open competition to create this institution together with exhibition designer GSM Project and museum consultant the Natural History Museum, London. The museum is located within the National University of Singapore (NUS), and sits next to the University Cultural Centre and the Yong Siew Toh Conservatory of Music. This context became a valuable opportunity to connect all three buildings and reinforce the area's role as the university's cultural hub, where science, art and music meet.

To relate architecturally to these other institutions, which open onto Alice Lee Plaza, our design adopted a similar typology to that employed for their buildings, with a structure placed atop a platform. In addition, the museum has a landscape deck spanning across the road that separates it from the other two buildings. This connection to the plaza ties all three institutions together with a common ground plane. The landscape deck covers the entire footprint of the site and forms the roof of the 2,500-square-metre (27,000-square-foot) principal exhibition hall on the ground. Sitting on the deck is the main building of the museum, which is conceived as a "moss-covered rock".

This distinct form came out of considerations around the building's performance. There are practically no windows, except for those indicating labs, offices or fire escapes, so as to shield the collection of over 500,000 specimens from natural light. This tomb-like environment sits above a gallery that requires a triple-volume void to house the fossils of three diplodocid sauropod dinosaurs. The need for future expansion has also shaped the building's massing. On the east of the site, space was set aside to allow the single-storey Education and Outreach wing to be extended upwards with four additional floors when required. We were left with a compact and solid building mass, a form that we then envisioned as a monolithic rock. This geological allegory is expressed externally as a mass of off-form concrete stained with a mineral silicate. To soften this austere appearance, the front facade is cleaved to reveal native plants that reference the sea cliffs of coastal Singapore. A 500-square-metre (5,400-square-foot) courtyard between the main building and the wing also serves as a garden for teaching the histories of both local mangrove swamps and plant life on earth.

02

01 OPPOSITE The museum is a landmark within the National University of Singapore campus.

02 Rear view of the museum.

03

03 The museum sits on an elevated landscape deck,
accessible via a grand stairway. A bridge connects
it to the Alice Lee Plaza across the road.

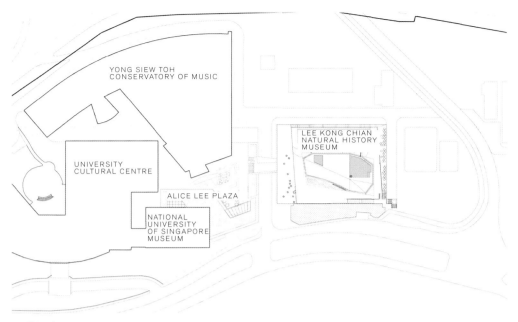

YONG SIEW TOH
CONSERVATORY OF MUSIC

UNIVERSITY
CULTURAL CENTRE

LEE KONG CHIAN
NATURAL HISTORY
MUSEUM

ALICE LEE PLAZA

NATIONAL
UNIVERSITY
OF SINGAPORE
MUSEUM

Site plan

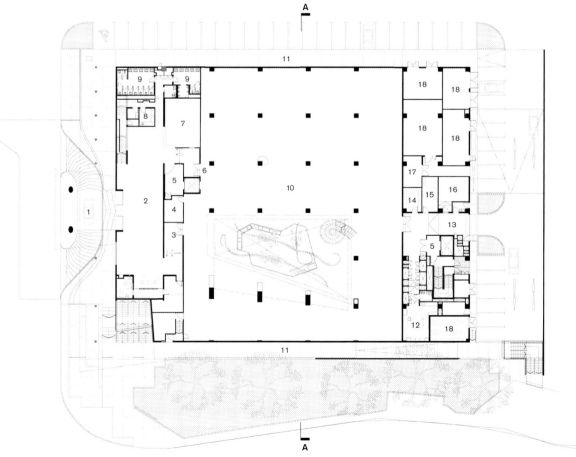

A

Lower 1st storey

1	Drop off
2	Main lobby
3	Exhibition entrance
4	Store
5	Lift lobby
6	Exhibition exit
7	Shop
8	Nursing room
9	Toilets
10	Gallery
11	Arcade
12	Workshop
13	Loading bay
14	Animal holding area
15	Freezer
16	Field store
17	Domestic room
18	M&E spaces
19	Bridge
20	Covered walkway
21	Open plaza
22	Lobby
23	Heritage gallery

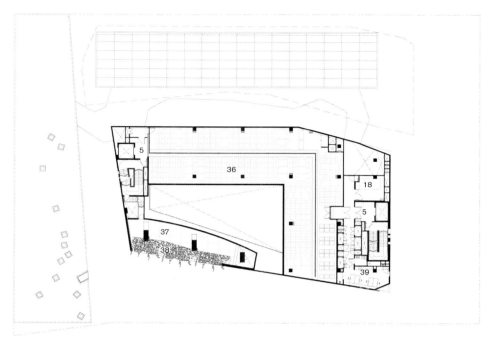

2nd storey

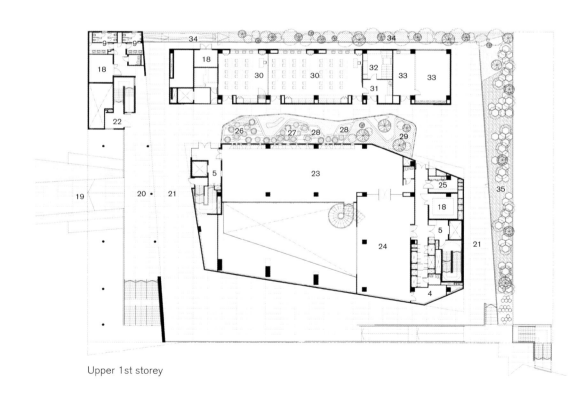

24 Temporary gallery
25 Pantry
26 Salt-water
    mangrove planter
27 Fresh-water
    mangrove planter
28 Investigative pond
29 Dryland forest
30 Classroom
31 Preparation room/
    volunteer room
32 Teaching-collection space
33 Bachelor of environmental
    studies room
34 Beach landscape
35 Phylogenetic garden
36 Wet collections
37 Maintenance ledge
38 Sea-cliff landscape
39 Lab
40 Dry collections
41 Office
42 Library

Upper 1st storey

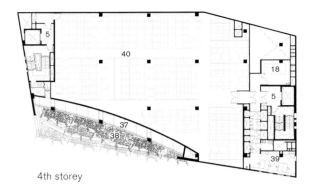

4th storey

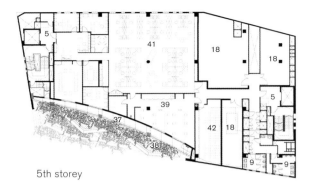

5th storey

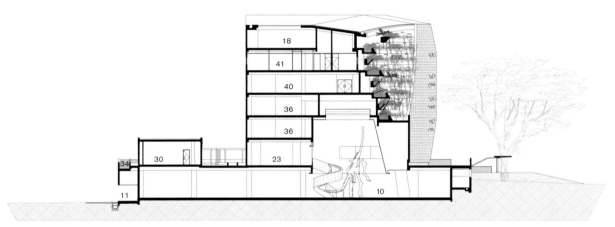

Section AA

1	Drop off	11	Arcade	21	Open plaza	29	Dryland forest	37	Maintenance ledge
2	Main lobby	12	Workshop	22	Lobby	30	Classroom	38	Sea-cliff landscape
3	Exhibition entrance	13	Loading bay	23	Heritage gallery	31	Preparation room/	39	Lab
4	Store	14	Animal holding area	24	Temporary gallery		volunteer room	40	Dry collections
5	Lift lobby	15	Freezer	25	Pantry	32	Teaching-collection space	41	Office
6	Exhibition exit	16	Field store	26	Salt-water	33	Bachelor of environmental	42	Library
7	Shop	17	Domestic room		mangrove planter		studies room		
8	Nursing room	18	M&E spaces	27	Fresh-water	34	Beach landscape		
9	Toilets	19	Bridge		mangrove planter	35	Phylogenetic garden		
10	Gallery	20	Covered walkway	28	Investigative pond	36	Wet collections		

04 The museum is skewed to channel views and movement towards the Yong Siew Toh Conservatory of Music.

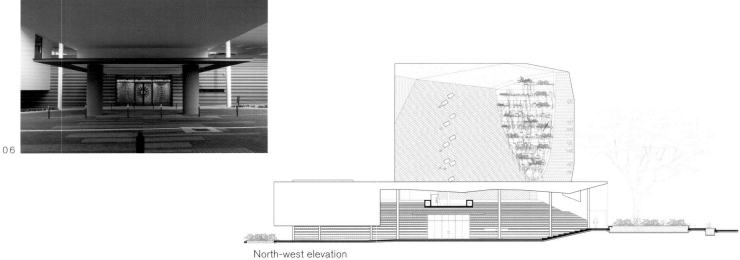

North-west elevation

05 Stairway leading up to the landscape deck.

06 Entrance to museum lobby.

07 The bridge between Alice Lee Plaza and the museum.

08 Arriving at the landscape deck via the connecting bridge.

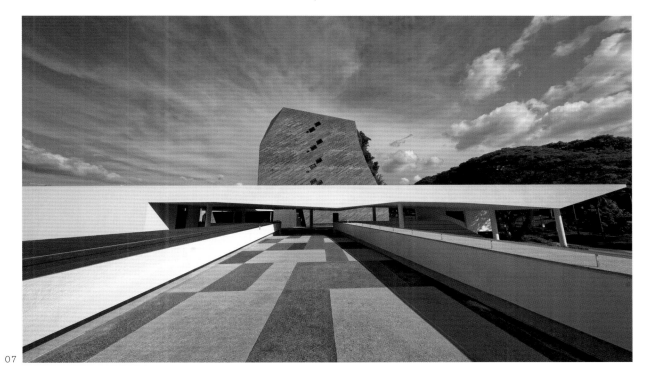

07

08

09 OVERLEAF The museum is conceived as a
"moss-covered rock".

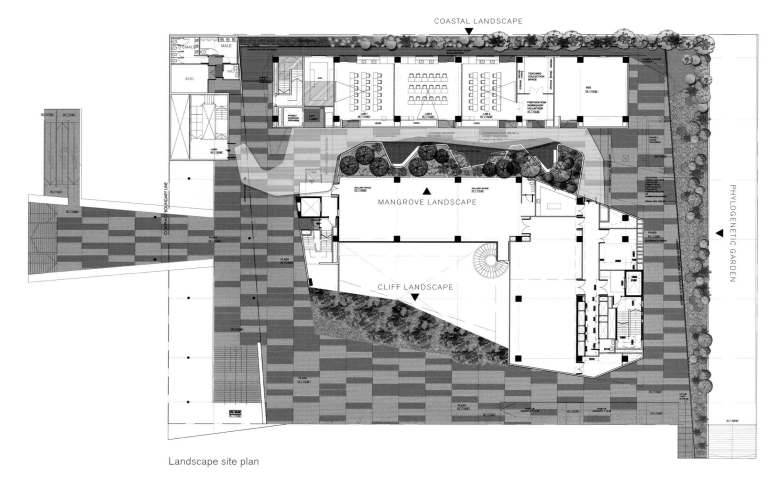

COASTAL LANDSCAPE ▼

PHYLOGENETIC GARDEN ▶

MANGROVE LANDSCAPE ▲

CLIFF LANDSCAPE ▼

Landscape site plan

10

10 The eastern edge of the deck features a phylogenetic garden.

11

12

11 & 12 The landscape on the facade references the sea cliffs of coastal Singapore.

13

14

15

13 Mangrove ponds are featured in the courtyard between the museum and the classroom block.

14 & 15 Openings on the facade allow views from inside the gallery to the mangrove ponds outside.

16

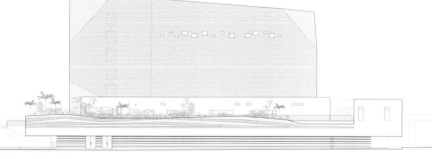

North-east elevation

16 Veranda alongside the mangrove ponds.

17 The northern edge of the deck features a coastal-themed landscape.

18 OVERLEAF A triple-volume space is carved out of the underside of the "rock" to house the dinosaurs.

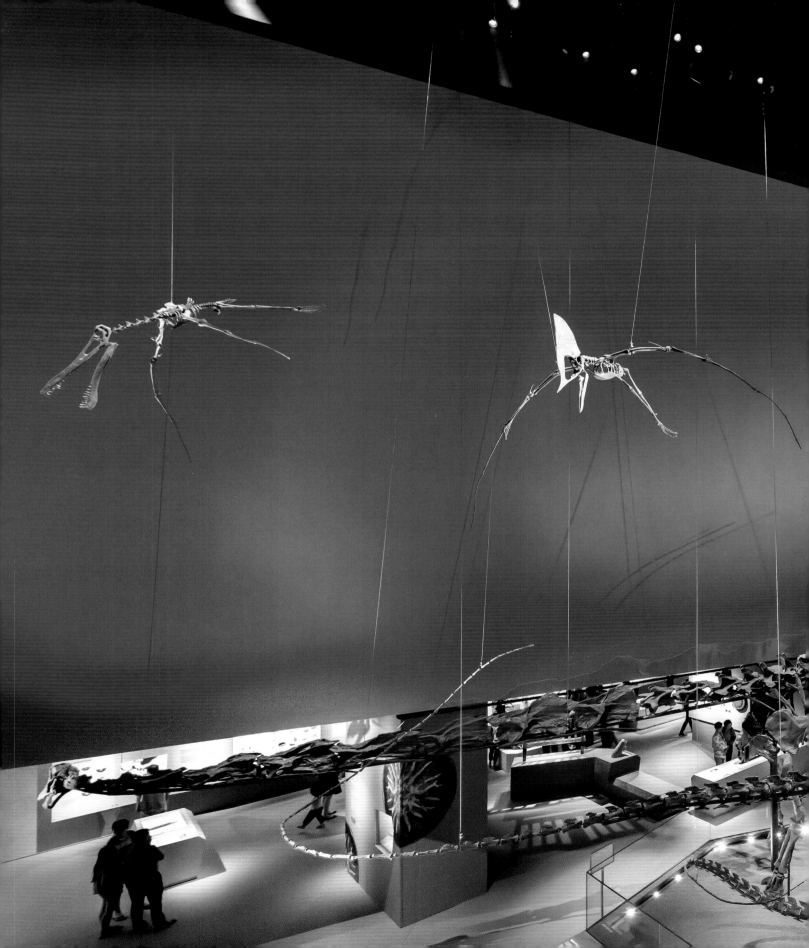

19

20

Alice Lee Plaza

After winning the museum project, we were commissioned separately to improve the plaza too. This important thoroughfare channels pedestrian flow from the University Town on the east of the museum towards the rest of this district. We introduced a lofty aluminium canopy supported on slender columns to shelter this previously hot and hostile space. The canopy also strategically frames views of the three different buildings. This not only gives an increased presence to the main entrance of the University Cultural Centre's NUS Museum, but also creates a formal drop-off point. Complete with a series of flagpoles, the porch offers a frontage for each of the three institutions to announce their different programmes.

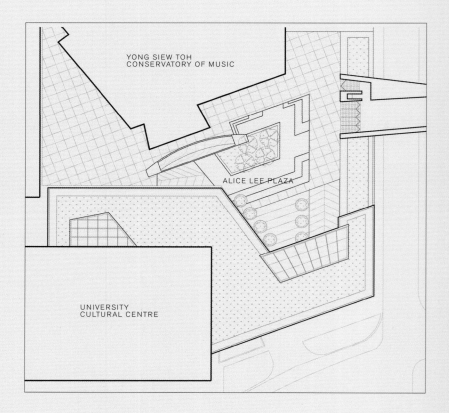

19 The lofty canopy shading the plaza also acts as a drop-off porch.

20 & 21 The canopy shades the previously exposed route to the NUS Museum. A skylight accentuates the museum entrance.

22 & 24 The canopy frames views of the cultural institutions around the plaza.

23 From Alice Lee Plaza, a flight of steps leads to the connecting bridge to Lee Kong Chian Natural History Museum.

21

22

23

24

ARCHITECTURE OF THE WEST AND THE EAST
REFRACTED THROUGH AN ARCHITECT IN SINGAPORE

By Leon van Schaik

There come times when we, members of the species *Homo sapiens*, pause to take stock. We do our mental house-keeping, dragging into a spotlight half-remembered achievements, setting them out in a new mental space and surprising ourselves with the order and coherence of our accomplishments. Mok Wei Wei, architect extraordinaire, friend and colleague of some decades, has entrained a few of us in such a stocktake.

I wondered, "What can an old friend do to assist in this spring-clean?" "Muse upon the ways in which people are seen to exist in the world," was my answer. Having had cause to review my own curriculum vitae recently, I was overtaken by the memory of travelling from Hong Kong to Macau on a high-speed hydrofoil ferry. Taking the sea as the medium of the journey – as time – I could see islands of achievement looming up ahead, coming into focus, offering up as we flashed past a moment of eidetic clarity: fisherman's shelter, cormorants drying their wings, an image that was almost immediately lost in the spray and wash of the ferry's wake. Island after island was passed in the same manner until the ferry slowed and we have arrived at our destination, the present time of that moment.

When we look back, our journey seems to have taken its inevitable course, but at each stage it encompassed acts of refraction, response and reflection, just as Mok Wei Wei's work is presented in this publication. It becomes a coherent journey when we, as is said, "join the dots". So, while looking at the broad sweep of a career, these "three Rs" give a useful structure; yet I know that when we look closely at any specific part of the journey, it will disaggregate into its islands of endeavour.

Why are such searches so interesting to us? Why is it, amidst so many such researches, so important that Wei Wei makes an exact account of his motives and interests? I come at this point to a vivid moment in a BBC documentary by physicist Brian Cox. "The universe is thirteen billion years old," he says, "and it has taken that long for consciousness to emerge within it, and we are that consciousness." So it is that the human project is the development of consciousness, a project in which we all have a part to play. But our civilization is very, very young. Five thousand years old. There are older civilizations. Aboriginal history in Australia stretches back 60,000 years, and predicates totally different concepts of our role in maintaining the balance of forces that sustain our planet. These are no less "conscious" than those of our civilization. And so much recent research tracks consciousness through all living things, from plankton to trees.[1] As our consciousness expands, we can see that in some ways ancient aboriginal civilizations can be seen to be more advanced than our own, as of course can aspects of ancient Chinese or Greek culture.[2] To be conscious is our planet's project. So to read of another being's consciousness within its culture is to build on our own core project, the pith of our being.

In a photograph taken by Lena Lim, she captures "three monkeys", all of us born in the year of the monkey at twelve-year intervals, at rest on a corner of Parc Güell in Barcelona in June 1999: Wei Wei to the left, myself in the middle and William Lim on the right. The two Singaporeans span a generation

1 Peter Wohlleben, *The Hidden Life of Trees: What They Feel, How They Communicate – Discoveries from a Secret World* (Melbourne: Black Inc., 2016).

2 Bill Gammage, *The Biggest Estate on Earth: How Aborigines Made Australia* (Sydney: Allen and Unwin, 2011).

but also a cultural divide. William was educated in Cantonese and Chinese; Wei Wei, unusually for a Singaporean, in Chinese. Their business lives have been conducted in English, though Wei Wei spoke Chinese at home, and William English. Completely ordinarily, although of Anglo-Dutch extraction, my life has been lived in English. Wei Wei's educational geography, while linguistically complex, was unitary: Singapore bounded his primary, secondary and tertiary experience. William's education had a lateral geography, stretching from Hong Kong to Singapore and on to the Architectural Association School of Architecture in London, and subsequently to postgraduate study at Harvard. My educational trajectory was longitudinal: early days in the southern hemisphere; secondary and tertiary in England; then postgraduate study commencing in the south and completing in the north.

What caused these variously complicated life pathways? All were set in motion by the slow expansion across the globe of European trade and technology. For all three of us, the major parts of our lives have been lived in an emergent "postcolonial" era, one that in its current phase has China resurgent on the world stage. This situates all of us in a flux of culture between East and West, and in particular places: Wei Wei pivoting from the fulcrum of Singapore, an island city-state that refracts all the cultures on the East–West continuum.

Threaded through any understanding of the condition of being in the world in these times are concepts of Modernism, some Western, some Eastern. The former tend to emphasize the individual as a focus of development and the normalization of individual rights; the latter have a collective advancement ethos that accepts a range of differences in the idea of rights and duties within a collective. These poles have preoccupied thinkers for 150 years: in the late nineteenth and early twentieth centuries the novelist Joseph Conrad – whose geography spanned the full range of ours (and more) – argued that what the West called "civilization" was in fact merely "material interest", an excuse for ruthless and savage exploitation, whereas in "the orient", "'three hundred miles beyond the end of telegraph cables and mail-boat lines' you could find a sort of honest authenticity that the West had long since abandoned."[3] Conrad looked at the actions of his compatriots with clear eyes, a critic of modernity as a rapacious economic system.

By contrast, architecture as a profession has been normalized through a vision of Modernism as a universal condition supported by a language, accessible to all, providing for all. Cultural differences were papered over as irrelevances. The fault lines in this early to mid-twentieth-century project were revealed in the two great European wars. Postmodernism reasserted the cultural but did not eschew the metropolitan centralism of the imperial construct. The individual as creator straddled this convention, despite the fact that architectural practice is necessarily a collective enterprise. As an individual, Wei Wei commenced his practitioner life working at first for William and soon in partnership with him. William Lim Associates became W Architects after William retired from the firm.

If we take the geography of the imagination into account, as I believe we must, there are necessarily two ways of locating these Singapore-based activities. They intertwine. One is to understand the history of the individual, while the other is to capture the relationships of the individuals with the various collectives that they have come from and now inhabit. How does a return to the belief that architects are creatures of their personal histories as much as if not more than of their inculcated ideologies impact on the way that practice is seen today? In a sense, we return to the foundations of Western Modernism. Conrad argued that people arrive at understandings through observation and experience over a long period, that it takes time before patterns that lurk below surfaces can be discerned. Walter Pater, the English theorist who in the late nineteenth century paved the way for the Modernist, stream-of-consciousness works of Marcel Proust and James Joyce, basing his thinking on recent scientific findings, argued that "our physical lives are made up of scientific processes and elemental forces in perpetual motion, 'renewed from moment to moment but parting sooner or later on their ways'. In the mind ... 'the whirlpool is still more rapid': a drift of perceptions, feelings, thoughts and memories, reduced to impressions 'unstable, flickering, inconstant', 'ringed round for each of us by that thick wall of personality'".[4]

It is in sympathy with this perception that I here focus on the literal standing points of the protagonists, all "weaving and unweaving" themselves, in Pater's words, in a world of global influences, well adrift in the nineteenth century; and now, in the twenty-first, impelled by the technologies of the information age. Indeed, during Wei Wei's initial review of the works of the practice, it became clear that his early interest in Chinese space and identity, and in Southeast-Asian indigenous cultures, recurred time and again in

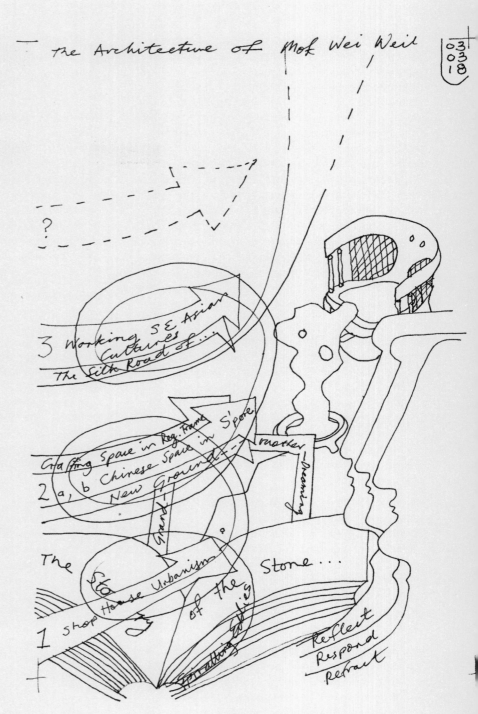

The Architecture of Mok Wei Wei

03
03
18

?

3 Working S E Asian Cultures / The Silk Road of...

Grafting Space in Reg. Frame / Chinese Space in S'pore

2 a, b / New Ground — Grand narrative — / mother — Dreaming

The

1 shop House Urbanism / of the / Stone...

Reflect / Respond / Retract

subsequent works. For example, he explored Chinese spaces in Morley Road House in the mid-1990s, and Beijing House in the mid-2000s – interests that were later overlaid with an involvement in the colonial legacy through the refurbishment of Neoclassical monuments. These concerns spiral through the works in counterpoint to the periods of development.

In Wei Wei's case, the "weaving" has sometimes been in isolation, always in counterpoint to collectives. His old friend Richard Ho became very much involved in the Rationalism of Aldo Rossi. Wei Wei avoided this, and also avoided the locally dominant "Tropical Architecture" agenda, with its emphasis on climate-responsive designs, which has now morphed into "sustainability design". Wei Wei writes: "This 'Tropical Architecture' narrative has dominated the Singapore discourse (as well as many postcolonial countries) since the 1950s. I think the unique (contra) position we take is worth emphasizing."

Recent thinking sees modernity as the (desperate) attempt to reconcile time as it is lived, one lifetime at a time, and cosmic time – the almost unimaginable *durée* that our individual lives nest within. Our broiling, information-age culture permeates newness, being avant-garde, being young or "emergent" – new on the scene. Thus those of us who are past middle-age face being examined as the producers of "late work", of coming after our early selves, after the new kids on the block.[5] But urgent and febrile as the pulsing of newness is, it nests, as observed above, within sweeping panoramas of time. Recently, after some decades of intellectual emphasis on forensic analysis of specific situations, panoramic histories in the mould of Arnold Toynbee's *A Study of History*, first published between 1934 and 1961, have become respectable again. Peter Frankopan and Walter Cohen are reawakening our awareness of the cultural continuum that stretches along the Silk Road, revealing how ideas and technologies have travelled along it in both directions for the duration of our five-thousand-year-old civilization.[6] Cohen argues that literature begins in Sumeria and Egypt and that as it passes along the Silk Road it spawns waves of literature in the East and the West. There are similar tides of influence in architecture, its technologies and ideas spreading along the trade routes – as I discovered when encountering the unusual hipped transept in the cathedral at Orcival as a young man. This architectural idea mysteriously floods the crossing of the church with light from a height that we do not expect to be there. And the idea can be tracked back along trade routes through the Mediterranean to Byzantium and Persia.

3 Maya Jasanoff, *The Dawn Watch: Joseph Conrad in a Global World* (New York: Penguin, 2017), pp. 147–48.

4 Annabelle Beaumont (ed.), "Introduction to 'Studies in the History of the Renaissance'", in *Complete Works of Walter Pater* (Hastings: Delphi Classics, 2017), unpaginated.

5 Joe Paul Kroll, "Sorry They're Late: Modernism's Permanent State of Being 'After'", *The Times Literary Supplement*, 5 January 2018, pp. 12–13.

6 Peter Frankopan, *The Silk Roads: A New History of the World* (London: Bloomsbury, 2015); Ben Hutchinson, "Empire Imposes Epic: The Global Influences on the Development of Literature in Europe", *The Times Literary Supplement*, 26 January 2018, pp. 24–25.

What is it that has led us to accept the nonsensical notion that we all exist in one instant, the electronic present? That what we do is directly and hierarchically related to that which is being done everywhere? Each of us weaves into existence a particular fragment of the culture of our time. This demands consideration in its own terms, not as a subaltern copy, as Rosie Llewellyn-Jones showed in her research into the ways in which Europeans at first marvelled at the architecture of Lucknow, and later characterized it as a poor, primitive copy of Western Classical architecture.[7] Over and over again, I have encountered this dynamic in the critical evaluation of architecture from what the recent and current imperial powers regard as the periphery: applause for mimicry, dismissal of difference. In fact, it is in the very acts of differentiation that the growth of architectural consciousness resides.

And so it is that, despite his resistance, I insist on talking about Wei Wei as a connoisseur. I observed Wei Wei in heated debate with a dealer in Colombo, arguing about the finer points of a "Burgomaster" chair: the height and curvature of the back, the length of the legs and the clarity of the carving. Why is he so concerned? In a way, these round chairs encapsulate a moment of collision and melding between Dutch culture and those in Batavia and Ceylon. These pieces therefore embody the Southeast-Asian condition.

Hanging in the offices of W Architects for some years now has been the enthralling *Grandmother Watching* (1988), a charcoal-on-paper drawing by Jimmy Ong. It is one of several Southeast-Asian art pieces collected by Wei Wei. He may protest that he is not a collector in the fullest sense, but these emblematic cultural icons find a place in his heart. Here is his response to an article I wrote about how architect Peter Corrigan was one such:

> First, I think most connoisseurs are collectors, but not all collectors are connoisseurs. By your lofty definition, I don't think I qualify to be a connoisseur. Neither am I a true collector because I often restrain myself from going all out to collect, as well as lacking the stamina to continue to collect. My motivation in looking at certain objects, besides being attracted by their aesthetic quality, is mainly to explore their social and cultural contents. So it does encompass both the political sense, as well the aesthetics.

> I am glad I am not an endogenous practitioner. I think the world is endlessly interesting. I like to be affected by it, and I like my creative impulses

to respond to it. It looks like I am what you would call an exogenous practitioner. But I should learn to be an exogenous connoisseur![8]

This is the extract to which Wei Wei was responding:

> Often encountered is the problem of what it is that lifts the work done by a professional out of the ordinary run of competence that professionalism entails. Having a view of what the good society might be and pursuing the expression in the work of that view is one modifier: the political sense. Another necessary modifier is connoisseurship: an exhaustive and comparative immersion in a field of human endeavour.[9]

Once entered, a connoisseurial field is an enduring resource, never fulfilled, always extending, always rewarding the attention paid. Some make their own work the subject of their connoisseurship, working in multiples and revisiting themes. This endogenous practice strengthens the work in its bones – the details improve exponentially, the readings becomes clearer and clearer. Reworked again and again, the work shakes down onto a surer and surer foundation. For all that, this approach has its problems. Self-quotation can replace speculation as the engine of work, and merely increasing the scale of a concept can take an idea beyond its capacity.

Exogenous connoisseurship – the obsessive examination of phenomena outside one's own purview – challenges (in the experimental sense of infecting) the endogenous. It is completely evident that Wei Wei is exogenous, that he is at ease in the world, aware of its doings and able to draw on them openly and creatively, as we see for example in his discussion of the influence of Frank Gehry on Church of Our Saviour (1985–87) and Tampines North Community Centre (1986–92), or of Jean Nouvel's Cartier Foundation (1994) on The Paterson Edge (1996–99). But this is in no way mimicry, it is applying architectural ideas to situations.

And in his collecting Wei Wei is in pursuit of ideas: the ideas of historic Chinese spatiality, the ideas of hybridity that arise in the diasporic cauldron of Southeast Asia. Wei Wei entitled his 2006 exhibition at Berlin's Aedes Gallery *Chinese More or Less*. In its catalogue he reveals how his sense of the Chinese emerged from reading and re-reading the Chinese classics, such as *The Story of the Stone* – not therefore from experience of Chinese space itself. He writes: "I did not visit a Chinese garden until 1988. My first visit was to Wang Si Yuan (Fisherman's

Net Garden) in Suzhou, China … walking through … the spatial sequences of the experience matched the wellspring of images in my mind."[10] Conversely, Malaysian born architect C. J. Lim, also a friend of mine, has brought an idealized England into existence in his writing and his utopian designing, while at the same time, more on Wei Wei's trajectory, he has given new form to the urban futures of China itself.[11]

The re-emergence of China as a world power has had paradoxical effects for Singaporeans of Chinese extraction, and for their sense of being Chinese. As Wei Wei remarks in conversation, a resurgent, successful nationalism makes the old patronising Anglo attitudes to Southeast Asia – "not quite England" – difficult to persist with. But at the same time it has marginalized the kinds of Chinese-ness that Singaporeans created while China struggled. As Wei Wei argues, claims to be culturally Chinese in a mainland sense are being replaced by the desire to differentiate a Chinese-ness specific to the local nationhood, politics and traditions of Singapore, and indeed of Hong Kong and Taiwan. The hybridity of Singaporean culture becomes starkly evident, as does its carriage through literatures and art. Embodying a culture through its literature has an ancient pedigree. Inflecting from the literature and the language, Wei Wei – see his Morley Road House (1996–99) – has embodied in his architecture a spatial Chinese-ness that eludes most China-based architects. Wei Wei, supported by many of his intellectual clients, welcomes however the release from categorization that the new Chinese situation has brought about, citing an article that begins: "What makes Chinese music Chinese?" and concludes, "In short, as everywhere else, national styles may or may not be present … among high-quality Chinese composers one can now find anything – and any level of 'Chinese-ness', including none."[12] In architecture we would eschew "style" and replace it with "spatiality" or "tectonic", but the sentiment holds true, and must be held in mind when examining this formidable body of work. Wei Wei's stocktake presents us with a unique insight into how a profoundly conscious and immensely creative architect can be both of his place and time, and of the globe and its history.

7 Rosie Llewellyn-Jones, *A Fatal Friend-ship: The Nawabs, the British and the City of Lucknow* (Delhi: Oxford University Press, 1985).

8 Personal correspondence with the author dated 24 August 2017.

9 Leon van Schaik, "Foreword", in *Building 8, Edmond and Corrigan at RMIT* (Melbourne: Schwarz Transition, 1996), pp. 8–12.

10 Mok Wei Wei (ed.), *Chinese More or Less: Mok Wei Wei + W Architects Singapore* (Berlin: Aedes Architecture Forum, 2006), unpaginated.

11 C. J. Lim, *Food City* (New York: Routledge, 2014).

12 Jacob Dreyer, "Composers of China with an Ear to the World", *New York Times*, 12 January 2018, p. 2.

1982–1984

**Goh's House,
98 Emerald Hill Road,
Singapore**

Featured project
See Chapter 1 pages 48 to 51

1982

**Bu Ye Tian,
Boat Quay,
Singapore**

Unbuilt

Featured project
See Chapter 1 pages 42 to 47

1983

**Chee's House,
5 Victoria Park Road,
Singapore**

Unbuilt

The first attempt at using a Postmodernist fragmented massing on a house, but with a vernacular form. This marked the beginning of the office's exploration of the "tropical bungalow" typology. The fragmented massing proved to be too experimental for the client.

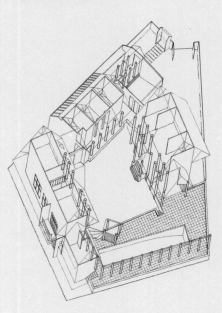

1985

**Residential Interior,
Thomson View Condominium,
Singapore**

This residential interior adopted a Postmodernist "Memphis" language, and was a precursor to Church of Our Saviour.

01

1985–1987
**Church of Our Saviour,
130 Margaret Drive,
Singapore**

Featured project
See Chapter 1 pages 52 to 55

1985–1987

**Saunders Road House,
54 Saunders Road,
Singapore**

This was a renovation to an Art Deco-style townhouse with beautiful terrazzo flooring. We kept the terrazzo floor and introduced new elements that engaged with it – similar to the approach taken with Church of Our Saviour.

1986–1989

**Tampines North Community Centre,
2 Tampines Street 41,
Singapore**

Featured project
See Chapter 1 pages 56 to 59

1987–1989

**Eng Neo Avenue House,
122 Eng Neo Avenue,
Singapore**

1987–1989

Scotts Shopping Centre Renovation, 6 Scotts Road, Singapore

Over the years, we worked on a series of major interior renovations for this popular shopping centre situated along Scotts Road, all while it was fully operational. This was a good lesson in managing a complex project.

1988–1991

Trevose Crescent House, 16 Trevose Crescent, Singapore

An addition and alteration to an existing house that introduced a small courtyard between two new blocks, bringing greenery and light into the heart of the house. A continuation of our "tropical bungalow" design exploration.

1988–1991

54, 58 and 67 Boat Quay and 29 Circular Road Shophouses, Singapore

The Bu Ye Tian project proposing an integrated conservation development was not accepted in totality by the government. Instead, individual owners were encouraged to conserve and refurbish their properties after the government announced the gazetting of the shophouses. With that, we had the opportunity to refurbish a series of shophouses for various property owners.

1989

Cameron Highlands Hotel, Cameron Highlands, Malaysia

Unbuilt

A boutique hotel at Cameron Highlands. The client loved the design but was not convinced that the project was financially feasible.

02

1990–1993

76 Emerald Hill Townhouse, Singapore

In this conserved townhouse, due to the drop in level at the rear, we managed to compact most of the spatial requirements in the new rear addition. This allowed the spaces of the original house to retain their generous proportions.

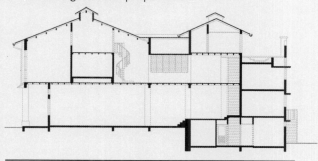

1990

Kemang Serviced Apartments, Jakarta, Indonesia

Unbuilt

The design of this development consists of two parts: a low-rise and a mid-rise block separated by a garden. The low-rise component consists of a rectilinear block and three free-standing structures that are held together in turn by an arc-shaped atrium.

The mid-rise component is essentially a slab block that is broken into four smaller "towers" with connecting corridors.

This scheme reflects the office's continuing fascination with fragmented massing.

 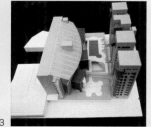
03   04

1990–1992

Tampines North Community Centre Extension, 2 Tampines Street 41, Singapore

Featured project
See Chapter 1 pages 56 to 59

1990

Peter Kor Studio,
Scotts Shopping Centre,
Singapore

The beginning of many boutiques involving the creation of a shop identity that reflected the fashion designer's style. The minimalism of Peter Kor's designs was reflected in our Neomodernist interiors, an approach that was also beginning to emerge internationally, for example, in David Chipperfield's shop for Issey Miyake in London.

05

1990

MIX,
Le Meridien Shopping Arcade,
Singapore

A unique shop design that embodied the innovative retail concept of a T-shirt shop featuring a few basic styles in a rich variety of colours and materials.

Six back-lit easels showcasing the T-shirt styles were arranged symmetrically and set amidst the warm-hued "box" of the shop. Finished in varying textures of brown cement render, this created an atmosphere that was sleek and yet inviting at the same time.

This was given a full feature in the *Straits Times*, which rarely featured design articles at that time.

06

1990

Anne Klein II,
Le Meridien Shopping Arcade,
Singapore

Designed at around the same time as MIX for an international brand.

07

1990–1991

Man & His Woman,
Le Meridien Shopping Arcade,
Singapore

The flagship store of a multi-label boutique that carried imported international fashion brands. Notwithstanding its international content, we decided to inject a regional feel by incorporating traditional Southeast-Asian materials, for example, the Sarawakian mats that adorned the ceiling of the shop.

08

1991–1992

Singapore Apparel Centre,
Park Mall,
Singapore

Our efforts in creating shop identities for fashion labels culminated in the design of a department store that was set up to promote local fashion labels.

However, in the context of a departmental store that was filled with merchandise, we learnt that it was difficult to project a coherent identity.

1991–1993

Lem's House I, 82 Jalan Greja, Singapore

Our first Neomodernist house. The building appears somewhat heavy but the spaces are light and porous.

This was made possible by the use of folding partitions that opened up the indoor spaces to the outdoors, and by interweaving planting throughout the first storey.

09

1992

Esta, Parkmall, Singapore

Another boutique where we used Southeast-Asian artefacts – in this case traditional timber loom parts from Madura, Indonesia – to create a shop identity. The designer, Esther Tay, specialized in the modern interpretation of traditional clothes.

10

1992–1994

42 Club Street Townhouse, Singapore

1992–1994

Crowhurst Drive House, 16 Crowhurst Drive, Singapore

1992–1994

18 Blair Road Townhouse, Singapore

A townhouse renovation where we introduced a tiered garden in the open-to-sky courtyard, which separated the conserved house and the new-build at the rear.

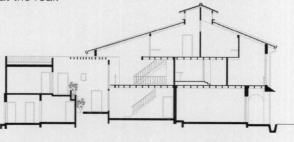

1993–1994

Nanyang Development Guide Plan, Singapore

In the 1990s, the government created a series of "detailed guide plans" to supplement the master plan. Many of these were tendered out to the private sector.

In our proposal for the Nanyang Development Guide Plan, a town centre was created that not only enhanced the facilities, but also built upon the existing cultural assets: in this case, the dragon kilns that were used for making traditional pottery.

1994–1999

Balam Road Public Housing Upgrading, Macpherson Estate, Singapore

In the 1990s, the government embarked on an upgrading programme for the older public-housing estates. In this proposal, besides meeting the standard provisions, we attempted to give the old Housing and Development Board flats a new look. This was done by extending and augmenting the simple Modernist facades of the old flats without resorting to the addition of ornaments to impart an identity. This was in keeping with our approach of respecting designs that reflected the conditions of their time, without erasing them in the process of upgrading.

11

1995–1997

**16 Everton Townhouse,
Singapore**

The renovation of this conserved townhouse retained and highlighted a few key original elements, while incorporating equally weighty new elements to interact with them.

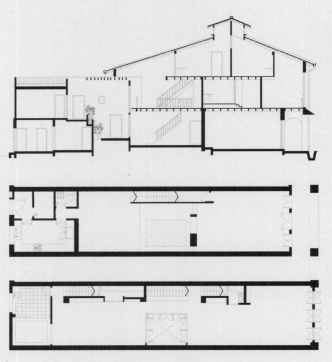

12

1995–1997

**Lem's House II,
Eastwood Way,
Singapore**

Featured project
See Chapter 1 pages 60 to 63

1995–1998

**Da Paolo Restaurant,
80 Club Street,
Singapore**

The refurbishment of this shophouse came complete with the interior design of the Italian restaurant. Various authentic artefacts such as old marble statues, old maps and even a marble mantelpiece were incorporated in the design, which adopted an overall language similar to that of Italian architect Carlo Scarpa, referencing the owner's Venetian origins.

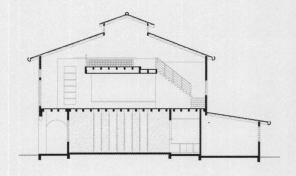

1995–1999

**Crane Road House,
37 Crane Road,
Singapore**

1996–1999

**Morley Road House,
4 Morley Road,
Singapore**

Featured project
See Chapter 3 pages 218 to 229

1996–1999

**The Paterson Edge,
26 Paterson Road,
Singapore**

Featured project
See Chapter 2 pages 73 to 79

1996–1999

**Petain Road Townhouses,
34, 38, 42 and 44 Petain Road,
Singapore**

We renovated these distinctive townhouses along
Petain Road, with a four-storey extension at the rear.

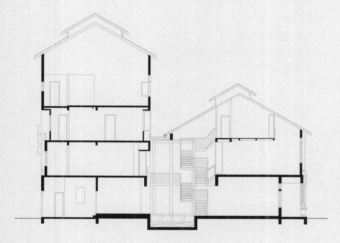

13

1996–2002

**The Loft,
22 Nassim Hill,
Singapore**

Featured project
See Chapter 2 pages 80 to 91

1997–1999

**Cairnhill Place Serviced Apartment,
15 Cairnhill Road,
Singapore**

This project was a renovation to convert a block of
existing apartments into serviced apartments, and
included all the interior-design work.

1997–2003

**The Arris,
28 Yan Kit Road,
Singapore**

Featured project
See Chapter 2 pages 92 to 103

1997–2005

**Toa Payoh Public Housing Upgrading,
Lorong 4, Toa Payoh Estate,
Singapore**

In this public housing upgrading project, we again
tried to introduce an impactful new element
to the facade while substantially retaining its
original character.

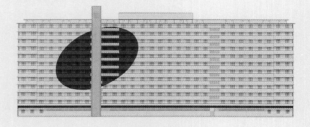

1998–2005

***Chinese More Or Less* Exhibition,
Chinese Heritage Centre,
Singapore**

Working with the writer Lynn Pan, who wrote
the script for this exhibition on Chinese diaspora,
we translated the narrative into a series of
spatial experiences.

14

1998–1999

**Da Paolo Restaurant,
56 Jalan Merah Saga,
Singapore**

1999–2001

**Ristorante Da Paolo e Judie,
81 Neil Road,
Singapore**

Featured project
See Chapter 3 pages 230 to 237

1999–2002

**Spottiswoode Park House,
68 Spottiswoode Park Road,
Singapore**

Featured project
See Chapter 3 pages 238 to 247

2000–2005

**The Trumps,
1 Jalan Kembangan,
Singapore**

Two residential towers connected by a low block are strategically located to capitalize on views and solar orientation, as well as to create a dialogue between themselves in the overall massing.

15

2000–2006

**Three Three Robin,
33 Robin Road,
Singapore**

Featured project
See Chapter 2 pages 104 to 115

2002

**GE Showroom,
9 Muthuraman Chetty Road,
Singapore**

2002–2004

**Chinkara I, II, III, IV and V,
UOB Plaza 2,
Singapore**

We started with the renovation of a single office unit for a financial company in the UOB Plaza. Eventually, the firm grew and occupied the entire floor, which we designed as well. Each unit's interior had a different theme tied together by a dark palette of finishes that alternated between textured and reflective, creating a sense of intrigue across the various spaces.

16

2002–2005

**Tanglin Residences,
23 St Martin's Drive,
Singapore**

This low-rise residential development consists of both townhouses and apartments.

The apartment blocks consist of four different unit sizes stacked up in such a way that the saleable area is maximized.

The townhouses are planned like a traditional shophouse, with a triple-height air well located at the centre of the plan that draws light into the whole unit.

The overall volumetric expression is set against linear elements such as the sun-shading and roof eaves, creating an intricate rhythm that takes on even greater complexity when viewed along the sinuous progression of the road.

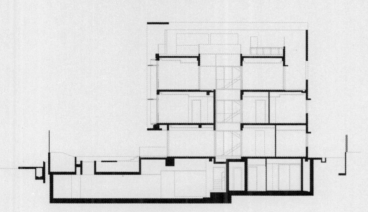

17

2002–2006

**National Museum of Singapore,
93 Stamford Road,
Singapore**

Featured project
See Chapter 3 pages 260 to 277

2002

**Miele Showroom,
163 Penang Road,
Singapore**

A polished interior that showcases the upmarket Miele appliances. The layout features a series of self-contained niches that isolate and give prominence to each displayed product.

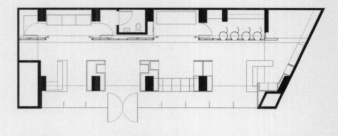

2004

**Beijing House,
Tong Zhou,
Beijing,
China**

Unbuilt

Featured project
See Chapter 3 pages 248 to 259

2004–2007

**Extension of Paya Lebar Methodist Girls'
Secondary School,
296 Lorong Ah Soo,
Singapore**

Featured project
See Chapter 2 pages 128 to 137

2004–2007

Camborne Road House,
16 Camborne Road,
Singapore

A large bungalow plot was subdivided into two smaller bungalows to house a multi-generational family. The small bungalow was for the daughter; within the larger bungalow we designed two self-contained houses for the parents and their son. A courtyard within this larger bungalow separates the two wings yet provides visual connectivity.

Through the crafting of spaces, the family can lead separate lives without intruding on each other's privacy, but are also able to come together to enjoy their shared spaces.

2004–2009

Riveredge,
21 Sampan Place,
Singapore

This L-shaped building is vertically stratified, with large apartments on the top three floors and smaller apartments on the middle tier, separated by a large sky terrace. On the ground-hugging tier, balconies that appear to slide horizontally engage the landscape deck.

A vertical cut-out spanning the entire height of the middle tier creates porosity in the massing, framing views and allowing for a breezeway.

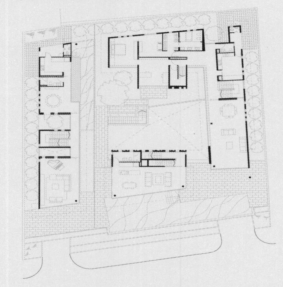

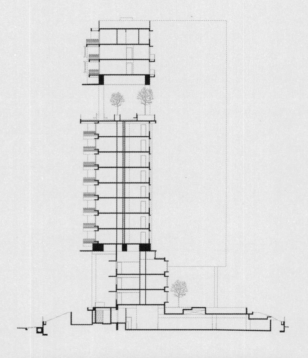

18

20

19

2004–2012

Katana II,
Jalan Ampang Hilir,
Kuala Lumpur, Malaysia

2005–2007

The 5 Legends,
Mountbatten Road,
Singapore

Chansville used to be the home of a famous sporting family in Singapore, and was conceived as a large multi-generational home. The 4,000-square-metre (43,000-square-foot) plot of land on which this conserved Modernist bungalow sits was subdivided to develop four smaller bungalows on one side, together with an extension to Chansville on the remaining plot.

The layouts of the smaller bungalows allow for views to their front gardens, while the rears look into water courts that double up as swimming pools. Together, the four houses form a chessboard-like layout interspersed with courtyard spaces that provide relief to the rather compact environment.

The two extended blocks at the rear of the conserved house are a self-contained family unit. They are tied back to the house by a stately double-volume dining room.

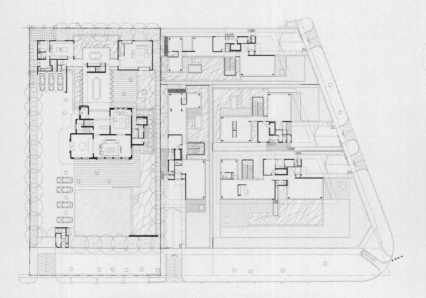

21

2005–2009

Cornwall Garden House,
22B Cornwall Garden,
Singapore

The house is planned on the principles of a Chinese garden, with its main entrance strategically positioned at the side of the plot. A series of spaces, each with its own landscaped view, is crafted from the entry point to the main garden, which looks out towards the front of the house.

A central courtyard, with a sculptural pine tree, is paved with patterns similar to those found in a classical Suzhou garden.

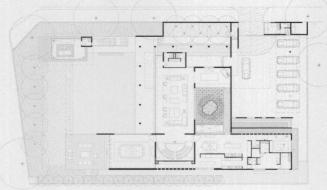

22

23

2005–2011

Holland Park House,
53 Holland Park,
Singapore

In response to a steep embankment at the rear that runs along the length of the rectangular plot, we created a bedroom wing that cuts into and sits at the foot of this embankment.

The L-shaped main house in the front is tied back to the bedroom wing, and looks back into an intimate courtyard that separates the two, and out towards an infinity pool that spans a substantial length of the frontage.

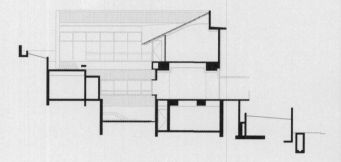

24

25

2005–2009

Peranakan Museum Exhibition,
39 Armenian Street,
Singapore

In the mid-2000s, the National Heritage Board set up a dedicated museum to showcase the lifestyle and culture of the Peranakan community. This museum was housed in a monument, the former Tao Nan School, which had previously been renovated with an extension in the mid-1990s to house the original, smaller Asian Civilisations Museum.

We were commissioned to work on the exhibition design. One of the highlights of this exhibition showcased the elaborate traditional Peranakan wedding ceremony, which lasts twelve days – this particular display occupied the entire second floor of the conserved building.

26

2006–2015

The Nassim,
18 Nassim Hill,
Singapore

Featured project
See Chapter 2 pages 116 to 127

2006–2009

Singapore Safety Driving Centre,
2 Woodlands Industrial Park,
Singapore

Featured project
See Chapter 2 pages 138 to 153

2006–2010

**Pathlight School,
5 Ang Mo Kio Avenue 10,
Singapore**

This is a school for children with autism. When we embarked on the project, we were faced with a lack of architectural literature to guide the planning of buildings for children with autism. We did our own primary research and proposed a layout with a clearly structured circulation. From the main spine, children are led into different sections of the school, each of which was designed with a distinct identity to enhance children's ability to register the spaces.

The greatest reward was finding out that, from the day the children shifted from their old school to the new one, they were able to settle and adapt into the new environment very naturally.

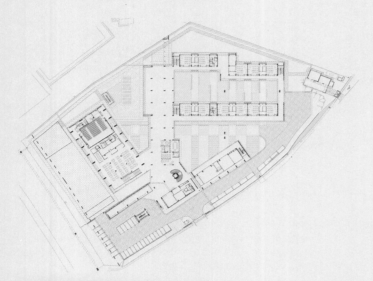

27

28

2006–2012

**Hilltops,
101 Cairnhill Circle,
Singapore**

As a result of the intensification of Cairnhill Circle, its numerous high-rise apartments created a very dense built environment. We proposed a slab block, with a shorter block extruded from it at one end. This created a generous communal groundscape with a large pool, which was a welcome relief for the development, as well as its neighbours.

29

30

2007–2009

**Triplet House,
64 Jalan Haji Alias,
Singapore**

We were intrigued by this family with triplets. The house's second storey was designed as an elevated plane that featured a cluster of bedrooms, with the master bedroom on the left, and three self-contained units for the triplets on the right. They are tied together by the family and study areas, along with an open-to-sky courtyard that features a frangipani tree.

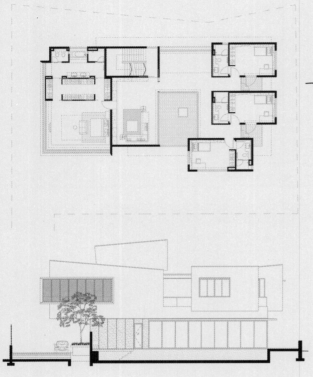

2007–2012

**The Party House,
137 Cove Drive,
Singapore**

Featured project
See Chapter 2 pages 166 to 181

2007–2013

**The Oliv,
11C Balmoral Road,
Singapore**

Featured project
See Chapter 2 pages 154 to 165

2007–2015

**Nepal Hill Master Plan,
Nepal Hill,
Singapore**

A hillock dotted with old houses built for colonial military personnel was to be master-planned to allow for intensification while conserving the houses and the unique topography. A mid-rise education campus anchored the corner of the site, while other new low-rise office buildings were sensitively inserted among the conserved houses and trees.

2008–2011

**Grundfos Singapore,
25 Jalan Tukang,
Singapore**

The regional headquarters and factory for the Danish company Grundfos, which is the biggest pump manufacturer in the world, consists of a long linear block housing the regional headquarters and a large storage/packing facility at the rear.

While the aesthetic used for the large facade areas of both these elements was planned with strict economy of means, a measure of luxury was created at the entrance, where a large water court greets visitors. We worked with the Danish firm Cowi to incorporate sustainable features, which was in line with the philosophy of Grundfos.

31

2008–2011

**Education Resource Centre,
National University of Singapore,
8 College Avenue West,
Singapore**

Featured project
See Chapter 2 page 182 to 197

2009–2013

**Swettenham Road House,
2 Swettenham Road,
Singapore**

Perched high in an exclusive neighbourhood, the house sits on 4,000 square metres (43,000 square feet) dotted with mature, conserved tembusu trees.

The entrance driveway ascends and winds along the side of the property, culminating at the drop-off porch at the highest point, creating a sense of processional grandeur. The house itself is planned around a central courtyard with the massing fragmented at the front lawn, creating the sense of a series of pavilions overlooking the gardens.

The swimming pool, strategically situated among a cluster of conserved trees, is perched at the edge of the lawn and overlooks the estate beyond.

2009–2014

**Victoria Theatre and Victoria Concert Hall,
9 Empress Place,
Singapore**

Featured project
See Chapter 3 pages 278 to 307

2010–2016

**Lloyd Sixtyfive,
65 Lloyd Road,
Singapore**

This development consists mainly of small maisonettes that feature a double-volume living room. The double-volume units are stacked on top of each other, giving a generous proportion to the north- and south-facing facades, while the block facing east and west is veiled by movable timber screens.

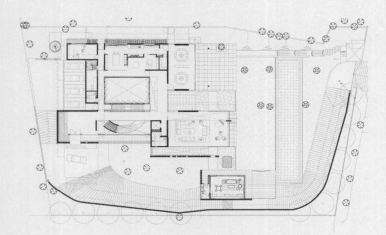

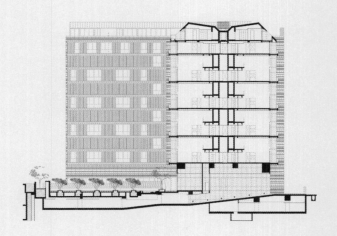

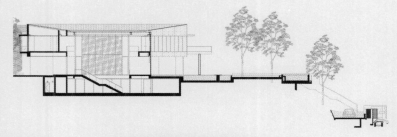

32

33

2010–2016

House I at Lermit Road, Singapore

Given the requirement to house extensive functions on their first storeys, the massings of the houses consist of larger ground floors that hug the ground, with courtyards to relieve their deep floor plates, and smaller massings on top that house the bedrooms.

The houses keep to a simple but sophisticated palette of finishes, forming a neutral backdrop, allowing the artworks and the layering of the spaces to be the main features.

2010–2016

House II at Lermit Road, Singapore

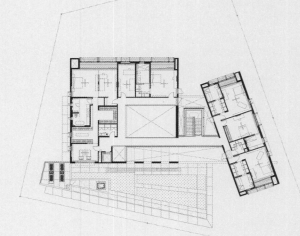

34

35

2011–2015

Lee Kong Chian Natural History Museum, National University of Singapore, 2 Conservatory Drive, Singapore

Featured project
See Chapter 3 pages 308 to 327

2012–2017

**Balmoral Apartments,
19 Balmoral Road,
Singapore**

This was a small development with units designed for rental and not for sale. In particular, elevated common areas that required additional maintenance effort were not desired.

The resultant massing consists of three small towers. Each tower houses a single unit on every floor. Two of the towers have white-painted surfaces, allowing the third brick-clad tower to stand out.

Together, the towers sit atop a large horizontal plane, below which are located the easy-to-maintain common facilities.

Interestingly, this development is two doors away from The Oliv, which shares the same plot size and configuration. However, the different briefs – the generous sky terraces that enhanced the saleability of The Oliv versus the minimizing of such provisions for ease of maintenance in Balmoral Apartments – have resulted in completely different solutions and architectural expressions.

36

2013–2018

**11 Kim Tian Road,
Singapore**

Featured project
See Chapter 2 pages 198 to 207

2013–2018

**Victoria Park Villas,
Coronation Road,
Singapore**

We master-planned this landed housing estate, including the design of the site section, which takes advantage of its steep contour. Within the context of a two-storey zone, this allowed an additional floor, which houses an on-grade parking garage and ancillary facilities.

To introduce diversity to the large development, we commissioned three architectural practices to design the houses.

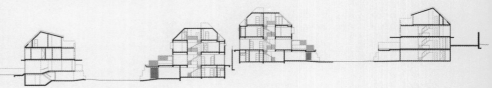

2016–2019

**Nim Collections,
Ang Mo Kio Avenue 5,
Singapore**

A large, landed housing estate that we master-planned, and where we also designed the houses. It employed a new set of envelope-control guidelines that gives flexibility to the design of the interior spaces within the envelope. The facade treatment has a faceted volumetric quality that capitalizes on every opportunity offered by the site to create variety within the large development.

2016–2019

**Maxwell Chambers Suites,
32 Maxwell Road,
Singapore**

A conserved building, which was formerly the traffic-police headquarters, was refurbished to supplement the function of the Maxwell Chambers, a mediation centre, across the road.

We proposed to remove a series of structures that occupied many of the courtyards, restoring the original spatial quality of the complex.

We also restored the facades, which were a curious mix of Neoclassical expressions externally, and stark Modernism internally.

At the centre of the long complex is a passageway that remains open twenty-four hours, as mandated by the planning authorities, and is treated with a palette of polished finishes that creates a contrasting ambience.

CHAPTER 1

CHINATOWN INFILL

Project Team: Mok Wei Wei

BU YE TIAN

Project Team: William Lim, Mok Wei Wei, Carl Larson, Richard Ho, Leong Koh Loy, Low Chwee Lye, Fung John Chye
Structural & Civil Engineer: Steen Consultants
Mechanical & Electrical Engineer: Preece Cardew & Rider
Quantity Surveyor: WT Partnership
Naval Architect: Kenton Marine
Economic Feasibility Consultant: SGV Goh Tan
Marketing Consultant: Johnny Loh Associates

GOH'S HOUSE

Project Team: William Lim, Mok Wei Wei, Fung John Chye, Leong Koh Loy
Structural & Civil Engineer: Steen Consultants
Mechanical & Electrical Engineer: Steen Consultants
Main Contractor: Techfield

CHURCH OF OUR SAVIOUR

Project Team: Mok Wei Wei, Leong Koh Loy, Daniel Wong, Toh Kim Sai, Lim Jin Geok, Yip Yuen Hong, Wong Mun Summ, Michael Chang
Structural & Civil Engineer: Steen Consultants
Mechanical & Electrical Engineer: Steen Consultants
Quantity Surveyor: Simon Lim Oh & Teo
Acoustics Consultant: CCW Acoustics
Main Contractor: Techfield

TAMPINES NORTH COMMUNITY CENTRE AND EXTENSION

Project Team: William Lim, Mok Wei Wei, Beh Ngiap Kim, Ong Chee Soon, Yap Kem Ling
Structural & Civil Engineer: Steen Consultants
Mechanical & Electrical Engineer: Steen Consultants
Quantity Surveyor: Rider Hunt Levett & Bailey
Main Contractor: Haxxon

LEM'S HOUSE II

Project Team: Mok Wei Wei, Andrew Chin, Bhaven Ravel
Structural & Civil Engineer: JS Tan & Associates
Mechanical & Electrical Engineer: AE & T Consultants
Quantity Surveyor: Barton Associates
Landscape Design: Tierra Design
Main Contractor: Teo Hee Lai Construction

CHAPTER 2

THE PATERSON EDGE

Project Team: Mok Wei Wei, Joan Loo, Johnson Lee, Susan Heng, Campbell Cumming, Mohd Zamri bin Arip, Billie Khoo
Structural & Civil Engineer: Steen Consultants
Mechanical & Electrical Engineer: Bescon Consulting Engineer
Quantity Surveyor: Rider Hunt Levett & Bailey
Landscape Design: Beh Two Design
Fire Protection Consultant: ABL Lim (FPC)
Facade Consultant: Curtain Wall Cladding & Design, Inc.
Main Contractor: Kian Hup Construction

THE LOFT

Project Team: Mok Wei Wei, Ng Weng Pan, Zhang Ying, Sanjay Lal Shrestha, Baet Yeok Hoon, Olive Siok, Mohd Zamri Arip, Wee Hiang Koon, Carol Cheng, Cheong Lip Khoon, Yau Yi Ting, Yeo Chian Ping, Stephanie Kuan
Structural & Civil Engineer: SCE Consultants
Mechanical & Electrical Engineer: Beca Carter Hollings & Ferner (SEA)
Quantity Surveyor: Davis Langdon & Seah Singapore
Landscape Design: Tierra Design
Lighting Design: Lighting Planner Associates (S)
Acoustics Consultant: Acviron Acoustics Consultants
Interior Design: Design Basis
Facade Consultant: ARUP Singapore
Main Contractor: Nakano Singapore

THE ARRIS

Project Team: Mok Wei Wei, Edmund Ng, Stephen Sargent, Cynthia Lim, Evelyn Ng
Structural & Civil Engineer: Web Structures
Mechanical & Electrical Engineer: Bescon Consulting Engineers
Quantity Surveyor: QS Partnership
Landscape Design: Tierra Design
Acoustics Consultant: Acviron Acoustics Consultants
Facade Consultant: Meinhardt Façade Technology
Main Contractor: Reliance Contractors

THREE THREE ROBIN

Project Team: Mok Wei Wei, Joan Loo, Nui Ratiwat, Carl Lim, Foo Yong Kai, Wagen Teh, Evelyn Ng
Structural & Civil Engineer: HCE Engineers Partnership
Mechanical & Electrical Engineer: Squire Mech
Quantity Surveyor: KPK Quantity Surveyors
Landscape Design: Sitetectonix
Main Contractor: Obayashi Corporation

THE NASSIM

Project Team: Mok Wei Wei, Ng Weng Pan, Foo Yong Kai, Darren Tan, Darren Loh, Ooi Chun Kai, Carl Lim, Chan Kwong Ming, Charles Vinta
Structural & Civil Engineer: P&T Consultants
Mechanical & Electrical Engineer: Beca Carter Hollings & Ferner (SEA)
Quantity Surveyor: Davis Langdon & Seah Singapore
Interior Design: Design Basis
Landscape Design: ICN Design International
Landscape Surveyors: How Huai Hoon Surveyors
Main Contractor: Shimizu Corporation Singapore Office

EXTENSION OF PAYA LEBAR METHODIST GIRLS' SECONDARY SCHOOL

Project Team: Mok Wei Wei, William Ng, Lee Kok Wah, Patrick Tan, Jessie Yee
Structural & Civil Engineer: TEG Engineering Consultants
Mechanical & Electrical Engineer: Conteem Engineers
Quantity Surveyor: Rider Levett Bucknall LLP
Acoustics Consultant: Acviron Acoustics Consultants
Main Contractor: Fonda Construction

SINGAPORE SAFETY DRIVING CENTRE

Project Team: Mok Wei Wei, Ng Weng Pan, Yeo Yih Hsiu, Foo Yong Kai, Darren Low, Chan Kwong Ming
Structural & Civil Engineer: Web Structures
Mechanical & Electrical Engineer: Bescon Consulting Engineers
Quantity Surveyor: Davis Langdon & Seah Singapore
Main Contractor: Chip Eng Seng Contractors (1988)

THE OLIV

Project Team: Mok Wei Wei, Joan Loo, Darren Tee, Ho Yenn Giin, Chan Kwong Ming, Roderic San Pedro
Structural & Civil Engineer: Tham & Wong LLP / TC Sin & Associates
Mechanical & Electrical Engineer: Elead Associates
Quantity Surveyor: PQS Consultants
Landscape Design: ICN Design International
Main Contractor: Thye Chuan Engineering Const. Co.

CHAPTER 3

THE PARTY HOUSE

Project Team: Mok Wei Wei, Darren Tan, Suchada Kasemsap, Patrick Tan, Chan Kwong Ming, Roderic San Pedro
Structural & Civil Engineer: JS Tan & Associates
Mechanical & Electrical Engineer: AE & T Consultants
Quantity Surveyor: Barton Associates
Interior Design (FF & E): Design Basis
Landscape Design: Salad Dressing
Main Contractor: Daiya Engineering & Construction

EDUCATION RESOURCE CENTRE

Project Team: Mok Wei Wei, Ng Weng Pan, Darren Tee, Foo Yong Kai, Darren Tan, Ekkachan Eiamananwattana, Chanon Petchsangngam, Jonathan Chua, Wong Shu Jun, Chan Kwong Ming, Roderic San Pedro, Carlo Montoya
Project Manager: SIPM Consultants
Structural & Civil Engineer: TYLin International
Mechanical & Electrical Engineer: Parsons Brinkerhoff
Quantity Surveyor: Surbana Int'l Consult. / Rider Levett Bucknall LLP
Lighting Design: Lighting Planner Associates (S)
Acoustics Consultant: Aviron Acoustics Consultants
Interior Design: Design Basis
ESD Consultant: COWI A/S
Water Irrigation Consultant: Christensen Irrigation (Singapore)
Arborist: Arborculture
Security Consultant: Certis CISCO Security
Main Contractor: Kim Seng Heng Engineering Construction

11 KIM TIAN ROAD

Project Team: Mok Wei Wei, Ng Weng Pan, Joanne Goh, Watcharapol Taemeyachat, Darren Tan, Darren Tee, Tan You Jie, Chew Zi Yan, Chan Kwong Ming, Roderic San Pedro
Structural & Civil Engineer: KTP Consultants
Mechanical & Electrical Engineer: ARUP Singapore
Quantity Surveyor: Rider Levett Bucknall LLP
Lighting Design: Meinhardt Light Studio
Traffic Consultant: TCP Solutions
Car Park Consultant: TSM Consultancy
Green Mark Consultant: ARUP Singapore
Landscape Design: Coen Design International
Interior Design: Design Basis
Land Surveyor: Tang Tuck Kim Registered Surveyor
Main Contractor: Tiong Aik Construction

MORLEY ROAD HOUSE

Project Team: Mok Wei Wei, Joan Loo, Billie Khoo, John Soo, Susan Heng
Structural & Civil Engineer: HK Low & Associates
Mechanical & Electrical Engineer: AE & T Consultants
Quantity Surveyor: Barton Associates
Landscape Design: Tierra Design
Main Contractor: Pekson Construction

RISTORANTE DA PAOLO E JUDIE

Project Team: Mok Wei Wei, Susan Heng, Edmund Ng, Yao Chin Leng
Structural & Civil Engineer: KL Cheong & Associates
Mechanical & Electrical Engineer: Bescon Consulting Engineers
Lighting Design: Lighting Planner Associates (S)
Main Contractor: Grandwork Interior

SPOTTISWOODE PARK HOUSE

Project Team: Mok Wei Wei, Nui Ratiwat, Foo Yong Kai, Stephanie Kuan
Structural & Civil Engineer: KL Cheong & Associates
Mechanical & Electrical Engineer: Kong Eng Electrical Engineering
Main Contractor: Maxway Construction

BEIJING HOUSE

Project Team: Mok Wei Wei, Stephanie Wan, Foo Yong Kai

NATIONAL MUSEUM OF SINGAPORE

Project Team: Mok Wei Wei, Goh Wei Kiat, Nui Ratiwat, Joan Loo, Tang Choon How
Executive Architect: CPG Consultants
Structural & Civil Engineer: CPG Consultants
Mechanical & Electrical Engineer: CPG Consultants
Quantity Surveyor: CPG Consultants
Lighting Design: Lighting Planner Associates (S)
Conservation Consultant: Architectural Restoration Consultants
Acoustic Consultant: CCW Associates
Facade Consultant: ARUP Singapore
Exhibition Design: GSM Design Exhibits
Landscape Design: Studio Steed
Main Contractor: Sato Kogyo (S)

VICTORIA THEATRE AND VICTORIA CONCERT HALL

Project Team: Mok Wei Wei, Ng Weng Pan, Stacy Cheang, Wong Shu Jun, Yuen Phuket, Chanon Petchsangngam, Ekkachan Eiamananwattana, Ng Yong Chin, Joanne Goh, Darryl Sim, Chan Kwong Ming, Roderic San Pedro, Marc Lobas, Gupta Chander Parkash
Project Manager: Rider Levett Bucknall LLP
Structural & Civil Engineer: TYLin International
Mechanical & Electrical Engineer: TYLin International
Quantity Surveyor: Rider Levett Bucknall LLP
Conservation Consultant: Architectural Restoration Consultants
Lighting Design: Lighting Planner Associates (S)
Theatre & Acoustics Consultant: ARUP Singapore
Facade Consultant: Meinhardt Façade Technology (S)
Security Consultant: Certis CISCO Security
Traffic Consultant: MRCagney
Green Mark Consultant: ARUP Singapore
Fire Engineering Consultant: ARUP Singapore
Signage Consultant: Duet Design
Main Contractor: Sato Kogyo (S)

LEE KONG CHIAN NATURAL HISTORY MUSEUM

Project Team: Mok Wei Wei, Ng Weng Pan, Micki Chua, Ekkachan Eiamananwattana, Foo Yong Kai, Stacy Cheang, Marcel Peter, Chan Kwong Ming, Christine Yap, Lin Zhen Ping, Charles Vinta
Project Manager: Quants Associates
Structural & Civil Engineer: TYLin International
Mechanical & Electrical Engineer: TYLin International
Quantity Surveyor: Quants Associates
Museum Consultant: Planning and Design Consulting
Exhibition Design: Gsmprjct Creation
Lighting Design: Lighting Planner Associates (S)
Acoustic Consultant: Aviron Acoustics Consultants
Security Consultant: Certis CISCO Security
Green Mark Consultant: ARUP Singapore
Landscape Design: Tierra Design
Safety Consultant: CH2M HILL Singapore Consulting
Main Contractor: Expand Construction

WRITERS' AND EDITOR'S BIOGRAPHIES

CHANG JIAT-HWEE

is Associate Professor of
Architecture at the National
University of Singapore, and the
author of *A Genealogy of Tropical
Architecture* (2016, awarded IPHS
Book Prize 2018). He was recently
awarded fellowships by the Canadian
Centre for Architecture, the Clark
Art Institute and the Rachel Carson
Center for Environment and Society.

LEON VAN SCHAIK

is Emeritus Professor of Architecture
at the Royal Melbourne Institute
of Technology (RMIT University).
He promotes local and international
architectures through practice-
based research and commissioning
architecture. His books include
Architecture in its Continuums
(2018), *Spatial Intelligence* (2008)
and, with Nigel Bertram, *Suburbia
Reimagined* (2018).

MOK WEI WEI

is the principal of W Architects,
a Singapore-based practice with
a critically acclaimed and widely
published body of works. He
studied at the National University
of Singapore and is a Professor
(Practice) of his alma mater.
He serves as a statutory board
member to multiple planning
agencies, and actively contributes
to the urban planning of Singapore.

JUSTIN ZHUANG

is a writer and researcher who sees
the world as designed. He has
written extensively about design
and urban life in Singapore for
magazines and in books, including
*Independence: The History of Graphic
Design in Singapore since the 1960s*
(2012) and *ByDesign: Singapore*,
(2019), a compilation on unexpected
local creativity.